I0116292

Truth and Lies

Philosophy of Ethics: The Series, Book 2

L. R. Caldwell

Reason and Reality Publishing

Truth and Lies: *Philosophy of Ethics: The Series,*

Book 2

Copyright © 2025 by L. R. Caldwell

All rights reserved. No part of this book may be reproduced, stored in a retrieval system, or transmitted in any form or by any means—electronic, mechanical, photocopying, recording, or otherwise—without the prior written permission of the publisher, except for brief quotations used in reviews or scholarly works.

Published by Reason and Reality Publishing

ISBN: 979-8-9992710-4-4

Orcid: 0009-0005-6487-9274
Printed in the United States of America

First Edition: 2025

Dedication

*To the philosophers
who refuse to trade truth
for persuasion.*

Chapter 1

Protagoras and the Birth of Relativism

The Sophists and Civic Life

Protagoras of Abdera (c. 490–420 BCE) stands at the doorway of our subject. He was the most famous of the Sophists, the traveling teachers who trained citizens to argue in the assembly and in the courts. His short, striking claim, "Man is the measure of all things," became the seed of what we now call relativism. In this chapter, we will explain what he meant, how his teaching shaped a movement, and why Plato responded so strongly. The goal is simple: to show why Protagoras matters for the ethics of truth across history and for the debates we will face in later chapters, and yes, into modern times as well.

The Meaning of 'Man is the Measure'

The Sophists were not a formal school; they shared no creed and founded no academy. They were professional experts who charged fees to teach public speech, cross-examination, and practical reasoning for civic life. Athens—crowded assemblies, massive juries, constant lawsuits—created demand for this new expertise, and Protagoras became its emblem. In Plato's dialogue Protagoras, he even presents himself as one who openly claimed the title "sophist" and taught people how to deliberate well about private and public affairs. That mix of practical training and big ideas is the bridge between Protagoras the teacher and Protagoras the philosopher.

What, then, does "man is the measure" mean? In Plato's Theaetetus (152a), the slogan is reported and debated: truth—at least about how things appear—is relative to the perceiver. If the wind feels cold to me and warm to you, each judgment is "true" for the one who experiences it. Protagoras' position, as presented by Plato, shifts attention from an objective fact "out there" to the human context that judges and uses claims. Whether we read it as a theory about perception or a broader stance about knowledge, the pivot is clear: human beings set the standard.

Relativism and Expertise
Protagoras likely did not mean "anything goes." Even in Plato's retelling, he distinguishes between appearances that are merely different and judgments that can be made better through expertise. Doctors can help the sick form "better" perceptions, and skilled orators can help a city adopt "better" policies—even if "truth" still rides on what seems right to those persons or that city. This opens a path from subjectivity to public judgment: not a denial of improvement, but a claim that improvement is measured from within human needs and uses.

Law and Justice as Human Convention

Protagoras also advanced a conventional account of justice. Law, he suggests, is a human achievement that grows with civilization; justice is tied to what communities establish and maintain together. On this view, law is not a transcript of divine order but a shared craft of living—something we can teach, learn, and reform. That idea resonated with Athenian democracy, where citizens argued over what would count as just for the city. The Sophist becomes, in this light, a civic educator.

Protagoras on the Gods

Another famous fragment attributed to Protagoras concerns the gods: "Concerning the gods, I am not able to know that they exist or that they do not exist…" This is not atheism but agnosticism, an admission of the limits of human knowledge, grounded in the obscurity of the subject and the shortness of life.

The stance fits his measure-doctrine: claims about the highest things are still weighed by human capacities. That caution about ultimate truth will matter when we later compare religious, political, and scientific truth-claims.

Sophistic Methods and Double Arguments

The "group" around him—the Sophists—varied widely (Gorgias, Hippias, Prodicus, Antiphon, and others), but certain methods recur. They practiced antilogikē or "double arguments" (dissoi logoi): examining both sides of a question to sharpen judgment and expose hidden assumptions.

This was not mere trickery; it was training for a world where juries and assemblies had to decide without an oracle. Learning to argue both sides cultivates intellectual flexibility—and, if misused, can blur the line between seeking truth and merely winning. We will track both outcomes in this book.

Plato's Critique of Protagoras
Why did Plato push back so hard? If truth is always "for me" or "for us," then the doctrine seems to refute itself: when someone says "relativism is false," that too would be "true for them." Plato's Theaetetus develops this charge and presses a deeper worry: if perception sets the standard, how can we account for error, teaching, or expertise at all?

His answer is to recover a standard beyond mere appearance—a path that will lead to stronger accounts of knowledge and, by extension, truthfulness. We introduce the tension here; we will return to it when we examine propaganda.

Protagoras in Democratic Athens
Still, Plato's own presentation shows the attraction of Protagoras' stance in democratic life. When many citizens must decide together, what "is" just often

becomes what they can be persuaded to accept as just. The Sophists professionalized that persuasion. In the courts and assemblies of Athens, success turned on reasons that sounded credible to ordinary hearers. Protagoras' legacy, then, is not only a theory about truth but a social reality: a public sphere where speech creates outcomes.

Ethical Implications of Relativism

This is precisely why Protagoras matters for ethics. If communities are the "measure" of right and wrong, then standards shift with culture and power. That creates room for reform—but also for manipulation. Teaching citizens to argue well can uplift public life; teaching them to win at any cost can corrode it. The line between education and sophistry will be one of our running themes.

Sources and Reliability

To keep our analysis sober, we must separate reliable testimony from rumor. Much of what we know about Protagoras comes through Plato and later doxographers; his own works survive only in fragments and reports. Scholarly reconstructions therefore proceed cautiously: they draw from Platonic dialogues (Protagoras, Theaetetus), from Diogenes Laertius, from Sextus Empiricus, and from fragment collections. Throughout this book, we will cite such sources explicitly and avoid stretching them beyond what they can bear.

Three Anchors for Later Chapters

For our purposes, three ideas will anchor later chapters. First, truth as "what appears" to individuals and cities (measure-doctrine). Second, justice as a human convention shaped by persuasion (the civic craft).

Third, the educational method of arguing both sides (dissoi logoi). These ideas will let us draw a careful line between fair persuasion and deceptive rhetoric. They also let us compare classical Athens with modern media ecosystems without forcing the past into our categories.

Conclusion: Protagoras' Legacy

In short, Protagoras gives us a usable map. He shows how truth and ethics take shape inside human practice—and how that practice can be taught, refined, and, at times, exploited. Plato's criticisms will sharpen the edges, but they will not erase the point that civic life depends on speech and judgment.

Keep this chapter in mind as we study propaganda, post-truth politics, and the responsibilities of citizens and institutions. We begin with Protagoras so that, later, we can tell the difference between principled persuasion and the machinery of lies.

Endnotes

1. Plato, Theaetetus 151–160 (esp. 152a–c) for the "man is the measure" discussion.

2. Plato, Protagoras 320d–329d for the civic account of justice.

3. Diogenes Laertius, Lives of Eminent Philosophers IX.51 on Protagoras' agnosticism.

4. G. B. Kerferd, The Sophistic Movement (Cambridge University Press, 1981) for Sophistic methods and context.

5. C. C. W. Taylor, The Sophists (Cambridge University Press, 1976; updated in SEP entry)

Chapter 2

The Sophists and the Power of Rhetoric

The Centrality of Rhetoric in Athens

In democratic Athens, the ability to persuade was not an optional skill but a civic necessity. With citizen juries chosen by lot and assemblies of voters deciding laws and policy, speeches determined verdicts, reputations, and the direction of the polis. In this climate, oratory determined verdicts and policy.

The Sophists—professional teachers of rhetoric—rose to prominence by training citizens to wield language with force and finesse. Their methods reflected a conviction: in a society governed by debate, persuasion becomes a form of power comparable to wealth or arms.

The Sophistic Toolbox

The Sophists developed a flexible toolkit, blending appeals to character (ethos), reason (logos), and emotion (pathos). While Aristotle later codified these modes of persuasion, their practical use was already visible in Sophistic teaching.

Students learned invention, arrangement, memory, style, and delivery, and were drilled in adapting arguments to audience and occasion. One famous practice was antilogikē (double arguments), in which both sides of the same issue were argued to sharpen reasoning and reveal hidden assumptions. Admirers saw intellectual training; critics saw the schooling of duplicity.

Rhetoric in the Polis

The courts of Athens illustrate the stakes. Without professional lawyers to speak for them, citizens argued their own cases before large juries that could be swayed by timing, framing, and delivery as much as by facts. Sophistic training prepared litigants to anticipate counterpoints, exploit weaknesses, and adjust to the mood of the crowd. In the assembly, oratory could determine whether to go to war, levy taxes, or grant citizenship. The Sophists provided the training ground for this democratic combat.

The Ethics of Persuasion

This raised a central ethical question: was rhetoric a civic art or a corrupting craft? Protagoras defended rhetorical skill as essential for deliberation among free citizens. Yet critics argued that persuasion without commitment to truth is manipulation. When a gifted orator could sway a jury against justice or a demagogue could inflame a crowd, rhetoric seemed less like education and more like exploitation. The line between civic empowerment and sophistry became one of the most contested boundaries of Greek thought.

Plato's Suspicion

Plato gave classical expression to these anxieties. In Gorgias (463a–466a), Socrates classifies rhetoric as a branch of flattery—a skill that pleases rather than a craft that knows. The dialogue exposes the danger of elevating persuasion over truth: if citizens prize style above substance, the city's moral compass can be distorted. Plato's critique forced later thinkers to ask whether rhetoric can be disciplined to serve reason rather than subvert it.

Aristotle's Rehabilitation

Aristotle's response was to rehabilitate rhetoric as a neutral art: dangerous if abused, but indispensable when grounded in reason. He defines rhetoric as the capacity to discern, in any given case, the available means of persuasion. Properly practiced, rhetoric serves as public reasoning under conditions of disagreement, translating technical knowledge into arguments that non-specialists can assess. Aristotle thus concedes rhetoric's inevitability in civic life while insisting that it must be tethered to ethical character and sound inference.

Parallels in Rome

The Roman world carried forward and refined this inheritance. Cicero's De Oratore portrays eloquence as the crown of statesmanship: no leader could govern without the capacity to speak well. Quintilian later systematized rhetorical education and insisted that the true orator must also be a good person—vir bonus dicendi peritus, the "good man skilled in speaking." Roman theory thereby preserved the Greek ambivalence: admiration for rhetorical mastery coupled with fear of its corruption.

Medieval Echoes of the Double Argument

Centuries later, universities institutionalized disputation, a formal method of arguing both sides of a question before resolution. Though framed within Christian theology, the pattern echoed Sophistic practice. By requiring students to marshal opposing arguments, scholastic training produced both intellectual rigor and, at times, rhetorical sophistry. The legacy of antilogikē thus became embedded in the structure of Western education.

Renaissance Humanism and Civic Eloquence

In the Renaissance, rhetoric returned as a cornerstone of civic humanism. Scholars recovered and circulated classical handbooks; civic education emphasized eloquence as the companion of practical wisdom. Machiavelli, in turn, analyzed persuasion as an instrument of political survival, offering a clear-eyed view of appearances, performance, and power. The revival of classical models reinforced the tension first felt in Athens: rhetoric can elevate civic discourse—or degrade it into manipulation.

Civic Use and Civic Abuse

The Sophists bequeathed both a method and a dilemma. Their training empowered citizens to speak and deliberate, strengthening participation and accountability. Yet the same techniques also enabled demagoguery and deception. This duality will remain central to our inquiry: whether persuasion serves truth or erodes it. In this sense, the Sophists helped build not only rhetoric but also the enduring tension between truth and lies in political life.

From Athens to the Present

From Athens to Rome, from medieval disputation to Renaissance humanism, the Sophistic emphasis on rhetoric established persuasion as a permanent feature of public life. Words can bind communities or divide them, clarify truth or obscure it. That ambivalence explains why rhetoric remains both celebrated and distrusted in every age. As we proceed, we will see how techniques first taught by Sophists reappear in propaganda, mass media, and modern politics.

Bridge to Chapter 3

This chapter sets up the philosophical confrontation taken up next: Plato's suspicion that rhetoric subverts truth, and Aristotle's attempt to discipline it. Their debate will anchor our exploration of truth and lies in the chapters that follow.

Endnotes

1. 1. On mass juries by lot and Athenian institutions of deliberation, see Aristotle, *Athenian Constitution* 63; J. H. Kroll, "The Organization of the Athenian Dikasteria," in *Athenian Bronze Allotment Plates* (Harvard University Press, 1972), 69–90.

2. 2. On ethos/logos/pathos and the systematization of persuasive modes, see Aristotle, *Rhetoric* I.2 (1355b25–26). For *antilogikē*/dissoi logoi in Sophistic pedagogy, see G. B. Kerferd, *The Sophistic Movement* (Cambridge University Press, 1981) and the anonymous *Dissoi Logoi*.

3. 3. On Athenian court and self-representation before large juries, see Aristotle, *Athenian Constitution* 63; Mogens H. Hansen, *The Athenian Democracy in the Age of Demosthenes* (University of Oklahoma Press, 1999).

4. 4. For Protagoras and civic defenses of rhetoric, see Kerferd, *The Sophistic Movement*. For critiques, see Plato, *Gorgias* 463a–466a.

5. 5. Plato, *Gorgias* 463a–466a; Aristotle, *Rhetoric* I.2 (1355b).

6. 6. Alex J. Novikoff, *The Medieval Culture of Disputation* (University of Pennsylvania Press, 2013).

7. 7. Peter Mack, *A History of Renaissance Rhetoric, 1380–1620* (Oxford University Press, 2011); Niccolò Machiavelli, *The Prince*, ch. 18.

8. 8. George A. Kennedy, *Classical Rhetoric and Its Christian and Secular Tradition* (University of North Carolina Press, 1999).
9. 9. Mack, *A History of Renaissance Rhetoric*; Kennedy, *Classical Rhetoric* (1999).
10.10. Preview of Chapter 3 topics (Plato vs. Aristotle) keyed to *Gorgias* and *Rhetoric*

Chapter 3

Plato's Warning and Aristotle's Response

Plato's Warning: Relativism and Its Contradictions

Plato pushed hard against the idea that truth depends only on how things seem to each person. In the dialogue Theaetetus, he challenges the view often tied to Protagoras—the claim that a person is the measure of all things. If that were right, the statement "truth is relative" would itself only be an opinion, no stronger than its opposite. Plato used this point to show that radical relativism undercuts itself and leaves knowledge with no firm ground.

For Plato, this was not a narrow puzzle. It touched ethics and public life. If every group sets its own truth, then justice becomes a moving target and law turns into a contest of influence. In such a world, people are at risk of being led by speakers who charm rather than teach.

Plato's Gorgias: Rhetoric as Flattery

Plato sharpened the concern in Gorgias. There he compares true arts, like medicine and justice, with mere knacks that aim only to please. Rhetoric, when it ignores truth, acts like flattery, it wins approval without improving the soul. The danger is that citizens confuse persuasive style with wisdom and choose what sounds good over what is right.

Aristotle's Response: Truth as Correspondence
Aristotle accepted Plato's worry about relativism but answered it in a more direct way. In the Metaphysics he explains truth in simple terms: a claim is true when it matches how things are, and false when it does not. This view ties truth to reality rather than to shifting opinions. By grounding truth in the world itself, Aristotle gives knowledge a stable anchor.

Aristotle on Rhetoric in Civic Life
Aristotle also approached rhetoric differently. In the Rhetoric he defines it as the ability to find the persuasive means available in any situation. That definition does not praise manipulation; it recognizes that public life requires speech, reasons, and audience judgment. When guided by virtue, rhetoric helps citizens understand what is likely true and what action is best.

Seeds of an Ethical Divide
Plato and Aristotle therefore plant two enduring seeds. Plato warns that persuasion without principle is a threat to justice and to the search for real knowledge. Aristotle agrees that truth matters most, but he works to discipline rhetoric so it can serve reason. The ethical question that follows us into modern times is whether

persuasion should be treated mainly as a danger or as a tool to be trained.

Education and the Role of Rhetoric

Their different views of truth shaped how they thought people should be educated. Plato's model asks teachers to move students beyond opinion toward stable truths. He wanted future leaders trained to recognize lasting principles, not to chase crowds or trends. From this angle, rhetoric often distracts students from what matters most: learning to love what is true and good.

Aristotle kept truth at the center but built rhetoric into education. People must debate laws, judge evidence, and reach decisions together. So students should learn how arguments work, how character and emotion affect audiences, and how to speak responsibly. In short, teach rhetoric—but teach it with ethics, so speech serves the common good.

These two paths—Plato's insulation from rhetoric and Aristotle's cultivation of it—offer a practical choice for schools today. Either protect students from persuasive shortcuts so they can focus on first principles, or train them to use persuasion well so those principles can guide civic life. Both paths aim at truth; they disagree about how best to guard it.

Bridge to Chapter 4

The disagreement did not end in antiquity. Doubts about stable truth keep returning—through ancient skepticism, early modern debates, and modern ideas about perspective. Plato's warning and Aristotle's answer will remain our guideposts as we trace how relativism evolves and why the question still matters.

Endnotes

1. 1. Plato, Theaetetus 151e–152a, on Protagoras's "measure" doctrine and the self-refuting challenge.
2. 2. Plato, Gorgias 463a–466a; 500d–504e, on rhetoric as flattery and the contrast with genuine arts.
3. 3. Aristotle, Metaphysics IV.7 (1011b25), on truth as saying of what is that it is, and of what is not that it is not.
4. 4. Aristotle, Rhetoric I.2 (1355b), on rhetoric as the ability to find the available means of persuasion.
5. 5. G. B. Kerferd, The Sophistic Movement (Cambridge University Press, 1981), background on Protagoras and the Sophists.
6. 6. Christof Rapp, "Aristotle's Rhetoric," Stanford Encyclopedia of Philosophy (rev. ed.), overview of aims and methods of rhetoric

Chapter 4

Relativism Through the Ages

Ancient Skepticism: Doubt as a Discipline

After Plato and Aristotle, skepticism appeared in a more disciplined form. Pyrrhonian skeptics claimed that for any argument, an equally persuasive counterargument could be offered. When reasons balance in this way, the wise course is to withhold judgment rather than insist on certainty. This practice aimed at avoiding false confidence, not glorifying doubt itself.

Sextus Empiricus described this method with three linked principles: equipollence (the equal weight of opposing reasons), suspension of judgment (epoché), and the calm that follows (ataraxia). By declining to choose where the scales of reason hang evenly, the skeptic hopes to live without the turmoil of dogmatic conflict.

This differs from Protagoras's relativism. Protagoras argued that whatever seems true to each individual is true for that individual. The Pyrrhonist does not affirm all opinions as true; rather, the skeptic refrains from claiming truth where the evidence is evenly matched. Relativism accepts many truths; skepticism simply holds back from judgment.

Enlightenment Challenges: Hume and Kant

Together, Hume and Kant show two sides of the same challenge: Hume explains why unchecked certainty is dangerous, while Kant explains how reliable knowledge is still possible within human limits.

Immanuel Kant answered by turning the problem around. He claimed that the mind itself shapes experience. We never meet raw reality. Instead, we see it through the lenses of space and time, and we organize events with basic concepts such as causation. This framework makes science possible, but it also limits us. We know the world as it appears to us, not the world as it exists beyond our way of seeing.

David Hume argued that we cannot prove the link between cause and effect by pure reason. We expect the sun to rise tomorrow because it always has, but this trust comes from habit, not logic. He warned that human knowledge is less certain than we like to believe.

Nietzsche: Perspectivism and the Critique of Truth

By the nineteenth century, Friedrich Nietzsche pressed the debate further. He denied that anyone can step outside their perspective to see the world "as it really is." For him, every claim to knowledge grows out of human drives and cultural conditions. Knowing is always a matter of interpreting from within a point of view, never from nowhere.

Nietzsche also argued that language does not deliver a perfect picture of reality. Words sort different things under shared labels and smooth over distinctions that do not fit. What we call truth often reflects conventions and habits of speech rather than an exact match between thought and the world.

Still, Nietzsche did not claim that all views are equally strong. Some interpretations expose reality more honestly, support life more fully, or explain experience more clearly. Yet no interpretation can stand as the final, absolute truth. For Nietzsche, philosophy remains an ongoing contest of perspectives rather than a settled system of certainty.

Seeds for the Modern Debate

Each of these thinkers reshaped how later generations wrestled with truth. The Pyrrhonists urged caution when reasons balanced evenly. Hume showed that habit, not logic, underpins our confidence in the future. Kant explained how the mind itself lays down the framework for experience while admitting limits to what we can know. Nietzsche, finally, argued that there is only a perspectival seeing and knowing (GM III §12). Together, they remind us that claims to truth are never simple, yet they continue to shape modern debates about science and reason.

Bridge to Chapter 5

In Chapter 5 we will consider how modern science and contemporary philosophy respond to these challenges— from statistical methods that confront uncertainty to theories of truth that attempt to balance objectivity with the realities of interpretation.

Endnotes

1. Sextus Empiricus, Outlines of Pyrrhonism I.12 and I.25–30, on equipollence, epoché, and ataraxia.

2. David Hume, An Enquiry Concerning Human Understanding (1748), Sections IV–V, on habit and the problem of causation.

3. Immanuel Kant, Critique of Pure Reason (1781/1787), Transcendental Aesthetic and Analytic, on space, time, and categories.

4. Friedrich Nietzsche, "On Truth and Lies in a Nonmoral Sense" (1873), on language and concept-formation.

5. Friedrich Nietzsche, On the Genealogy of Morality III §12 and Beyond Good and Evil, on perspectivism and interpretation.

6. For general background, see the Stanford Encyclopedia of Philosophy entries on Ancient Skepticism, Hume, Kant, and Nietzsche

Chapter 5

Propaganda in History, the 1800s

Beyond the noise of headlines, the press started to do more than tell what happened; it influenced how people thought about events. Across the 1800s, propaganda became routine, woven into advertisements, editorials, pamphlets, sermons, and, most of all, the daily press.

A Sophistic Lens on Nineteenth-Century News

Labeling nineteenth-century editors as "Sophists" would be anachronistic, but the techniques rhyme. When information is abundant and attention scarce, success favors speakers who shape salience—what audiences notice first, retain longest, and regard as credible.

Urban and national papers constantly deployed strategies the classical Sophists would recognize: aggressive framing, stark contrasts between heroes and villains, repetition of vivid narratives, and appeals that prioritized impact over dispassion. The result was not the abandonment of truth but the redefinition of how publics encountered it: through rhetoric that filtered facts and guided judgment.

Protagoras, one of the most renowned Sophists, declared that 'man is the measure of all things.' This principle captures the relativism that nineteenth-century newspapers embodied. When editors framed a story, they were not abandoning truth but reshaping it to meet the perceptions of their audience. Just as the Sophists trained citizens to persuade juries and assemblies, editors trained readers to see the world through narratives crafted for maximum effect. What counted as credible was not an objective record but the version repeated with confidence and resonance.

The critical voices of the late nineteenth century echo Plato and Aristotle's ancient critiques of the Sophists. Plato warned that rhetoric untethered from truth risked manipulation, while Aristotle sought to discipline persuasion through logic and ethical appeal. Reformers who pushed for verification, attribution, and fairness in journalism carried forward that same impulse: to counterbalance the Sophistic temptation toward persuasion at any cost with a renewed demand for standards that preserved credibility.

This philosophical tension between persuasion and truth set the stage for the broader calls for reform that emerged in journalism at the close of the nineteenth century, linking ancient critiques to modern efforts to establish professional standards.

The Rise of Mass Persuasion in the Nineteenth Century

The nineteenth century altered the scale and speed of persuasion. Literacy expanded in both Europe and the United States, paper grew cheaper with wood-pulp production, and steam-powered cylinder and rotary presses turned out copies at rates no hand press could match. These changes pushed newspapers from elite circles into ordinary households, creating audiences large enough to move markets and elections. [1]

The Penny Press and a New Audience

Beginning in the 1830s, the so-called penny press sold newspapers at a price common laborers could afford. Publishers competed fiercely for attention, focusing on crime, human-interest stories, and timely political controversy. As circulation rose, editors learned that the tone and framing of a story could matter as much as the facts, and headlines began to do persuasive work of their own. [2]

Telegraph, Wire Services, and the Acceleration of News

Telegraph lines, adopted widely after mid-century, turned news into a near-real-time commodity. Wire services such as the Associated Press (founded in 1846) standardized and distributed reports across cities, allowing distant papers to publish the same dispatches within hours. Speed rewarded brevity and punch. It also made it easier for political actors to set a narrative early and watch it echo across regions before counter-messages could catch up. [3]

Pictures that Persuade: Illustrations and Cartoons

Wood engravings, later half-tone photographs, and editorial cartoons gave newspapers a visual rhetoric. An image on the front page could concentrate emotion— fear, outrage, pride—faster than a column of prose. Publishers learned to pair striking visuals with simplified storylines to guide readers toward a ready-made conclusion. [4]

Partisan Papers and the Blurred Line between Reporting and Advocacy

Much of the nineteenth-century press was openly partisan. Editors campaigned for candidates, promoted party platforms, and treated opponents with sarcasm or scorn. Readers did not expect detachment; they expected a champion. In such a climate, the same fact could be framed in very different ways, and repetition—rather than verification—often decided which version stuck. [5]

Yellow Journalism and the Spanish–American War

By the 1890s, rivalry between high-circulation New York papers helped crystallize a sensational style later called "yellow journalism." Publishers like William Randolph Hearst and Joseph Pulitzer discovered that bold headlines, crusading editorials, and dramatic artwork moved both copies and public sentiment. Coverage surrounding the 1898 explosion of the USS Maine in Havana Harbor showed how newspapers could frame uncertainty as urgency and channel outrage into political pressure—one of the century's clearest examples of media influence on foreign policy debate. [6]

European Currents and 1848
Across Europe, expanding literacy and cheaper print fueled a diverse press: party newspapers, religious weeklies, satirical magazines, and mass-circulation dailies. During the revolutions of 1848, pamphlets and papers accelerated the spread of ideas across borders. Authorities recognized the danger and attempted censorship, but the overall trend favored quicker publication, wider readership, and more organized persuasion. [7]

Techniques of Nineteenth-Century Propaganda
Common techniques included emotive headlines; selective statistics; repetition of memorable phrases; patriotic symbols; villains and heroes; and the use of authoritative voices—ministers, generals, scientists—to confer credibility. Newspapers also learned to shape public sentiment by commissioning polls, printing petitions, or highlighting letters to the editor that matched a preferred narrative. These methods became

commonplace in many twentieth-century practices in public relations and political campaigning. [8]

Backlash and Calls for Reform

Sensationalism triggered pushback. Readers, reformers, and some editors argued for professional standards and clearer separation between reporting and opinion. Late-century journalism schools and press associations began articulating norms—verification, attribution, and fairness—that would gain traction in the early 1900s. The backlash itself shows how persuasive power, once felt, invited demands for restraint. [9]

Endnotes

[1] For literacy expansion, inexpensive wood-pulp paper, and advances in printing technology, see Asa Briggs and Peter Burke, *A Social History of the Media: From Gutenberg to the Internet* (Polity, 2009), 157–163.

[2] On the penny press and its popular audience, see Michael Schudson, *Discovering the News: A Social History of American Newspapers* (Basic Books, 1978), 15–30.

[3] On the telegraph, wire services, and the founding of the Associated Press in 1846, see Menahem Blondheim, *News over the Wires: The Telegraph and the Flow of Public Information in America, 1844–1897* (Harvard University Press, 1994).

[4] For illustrated journalism and persuasive visuals, see Joshua Brown, *Beyond the Lines: Pictorial Reporting, Everyday Life, and the Crisis of Gilded Age America* (University of California Press, 2002).

[5] On partisan newspapers and the party press era, see Richard L. Kaplan, *Politics and the American Press: The Rise of Objectivity, 1865–1920* (Cambridge University Press, 2002).

[6] For yellow journalism, Hearst, Pulitzer, and the USS Maine, see W. Joseph Campbell, *Yellow Journalism: Puncturing the Myths, Defining the Legacies* (Praeger, 2001).

[7] On the press and the 1848 revolutions in Europe, see Jonathan Sperber, *The European Revolutions, 1848–1851* (Cambridge University Press, 2005), 85–110.

[8] For common techniques of nineteenth-century propaganda, see Philip M. Taylor, *Munitions of the Mind: A History of Propaganda from the Ancient World to the Present Era* (Manchester University Press, 2003), 173–190.

[9] On calls for reform and early journalism education, see Michael Schudson, *The Power of News* (Harvard University Press, 1995), 65–82.

[10] For the legacy of nineteenth-century mass persuasion, see James Curran and Jean Seaton, *Power Without Responsibility: Press, Broadcasting and the Internet in Britain* (Routledge, 2018), 44–5

Chapter 6

Goebbels and the Machinery of Lies

The Propaganda Minister

Appointed Reich Minister of Public Enlightenment and
Propaganda in March 1933, Joseph Goebbels moved
quickly to knit the press, radio, film, theater,
publishing, and staged ceremony into one coordinated
apparatus. Through licensing rules, pressure on editors,
reorganization of press services, and surveillance of
studios and stages, he pushed cultural Gleichschaltung.
Censorship and agenda-setting worked in tandem: some
topics were silenced, others were magnified without
pause. Under his direction, persuasion didn't decorate
power; it functioned as one of its main supports. [1].

Building a Single Voice: Press, Radio, Film, Spectacle

Party newspapers and compliant dailies sat at the
center. Goebbels had launched Der Angriff in 1927 as a
pugnacious Berlin sheet; after 1933, the Völkischer
Beobachter and allied papers supplied cues for
everyone else. Morning conferences aligned headlines
nationwide, and the DNB distributed uniform copy.

Radio carried the same tone into private rooms: the
low-cost Volksempfänger let millions hear speeches,
anthems, and bulletins that cast politics as simple moral
contrasts. Film reinforced the script. Newsreels and

features narrated unity, sacrifice, and enemies in ways that bypassed argument and targeted feeling. And mass theater—the Nuremberg rallies, torchlight marches, choreographed vows—turned politics into spectacle, where participation itself trained consent. [2][3][4] [See Endnote Volksempfänger].

Repetition, Simplicity, and Emotion

Nazi propagandists relied on a deliberately narrow formula. Complex realities were first reduced into stark opposites—revival versus collapse, order versus disorder, the German people against their alleged foes. Next came relentless repetition: identical slogans and themes circulated across newspapers, schoolrooms, speeches, and radio broadcasts until their very familiarity created the impression of truth.

Finally, emotional appeal outweighed rational debate. By evoking the humiliation of defeat in 1918, orchestrating vast public rituals, and presenting the nation as reborn, the regime stirred pride, fear, and resentment. Hitler demanded that propaganda revolve around a few essential themes endlessly repeated; Goebbels turned that principle into a systematic method across every medium under his control.

Truth, Contest, and the Collapse of Judgment

Plato warns that rhetoric severed from knowledge decays into flattery; Protagoras supplies a different brake—plural contest under civic norms. In the propaganda state, both brakes fail at once. There is no ascent to knowledge because inquiry is punished, and there is no contest because counter-speech lacks a platform. Speech ceases to be the place where claims meet resistance and becomes the instrument that organizes perception itself.

Once survival depends on echoing official phrases, the distinction between honest mistake and deliberate deceit dissolves. Citizens learn not only what to say but what can be noticed without penalty. The mental habit formed by genuine Sophistic exchange, listening for the stronger account among competing logoi—atrophies. In its place grows a performance reflex: recognize the cue, supply the chorus, and move on.

Manufacturing Consensus
Manufacturing consensus meant saturating the public sphere with one authorized version of events. Control of newspapers, film, and radio allowed Nazi leaders to blur the line between information and indoctrination. By monopolizing channels of communication, they left little room for competing views, training the public to experience propaganda not as an argument to be weighed but as the ordinary backdrop of daily life.

To manufacture consensus, the regime flooded public space with a single authorized account of events. Control of press, film, and radio blurred the line between information and indoctrination. By monopolizing communication channels, leaders left little oxygen for rival views, and citizens learned to treat propaganda not as a claim to weigh but as the everyday background of life.

Constructing Enemies and Wartime Narratives
A central task of Goebbels's ministry was constructing enemies. Anti-Semitic myths were repeated and elaborated: the Jew as international conspirator, cultural corrupter, and economic parasite. Bolshevism and "plutocratic" powers were cast as threats encircling Germany. During the late 1930s and the war years, propaganda blended news with fantasy, explaining setbacks as treachery and crimes as necessity.

Such narratives did not require universal belief to be effective; they needed only to define what could be said in public and to set the emotional baseline from which policy could proceed. This climate prepared ordinary citizens to accept exclusion, dispossession, violence, and eventually genocide as part of a story that claimed to defend the nation. [3][7].

A core assignment of the ministry was enemy-making. Anti-Jewish myths were repeated and embellished—the Jew cast as international plotter, cultural pollutant, and economic parasite. Bolshevism and the "plutocracies" were portrayed as encircling threats.

In the late 1930s and into the war, propaganda fused fact with fiction, explaining reverses as betrayal and crimes as necessity. Such stories did not need universal assent; they needed to set the boundaries of what could be said and to fix the emotional baseline from which policy moved. In that climate, exclusion, dispossession, violence, and ultimately genocide could be accepted as acts purportedly done in the nation's defense. [3][7].

The Assault on Truth

The deepest harm of Goebbels's system was to the idea of truth itself. If truth becomes whatever the state proclaims and repeats, language ceases to correspond to reality and begins to enforce it. Plato had warned that rhetoric cut loose from knowledge is a branch of flattery. In the Third Reich, flattery matured into domination: words did not merely describe; they organized experience. When officials call lies "necessary truths," and when citizens learn that survival requires repeating them, the distinction between error and deceit dissolves. The result is not simply a population that believes falsehoods but a public sphere in which reality yields to performance. [4][7].

The gravest damage fell on the concept of truth. When "truth" is whatever the state declares and repeats, words stop describing reality and begin enforcing it. Plato warned that rhetoric without knowledge devolves into flattery. Under the Third Reich, flattery hardened into domination: speech did not merely represent experience; it arranged it. When officials rename lies as "necessary truths" and survival depends on echoing them, the line between mistake and deceit disappears. What results is not only false belief but a public sphere in which performance overwhelms reality. [4][7].

A Sophistic Lens on Propaganda

Read through the lens of Protagoras and the Sophists, Goebbels illustrates how powerful—and how dangerous—rhetoric becomes when detached from ethical constraints. The Sophists taught that persuasion is central to civic life and that skilled speech can improve judgment. They trained citizens to use antilogikē (double arguments) so that opposing cases could be weighed in public. Goebbels inverted that ideal.

He preserved the Sophistic insight that speech shapes the city, but he replaced plural argument with monopolized narrative. Where Protagoras treated law and justice as human conventions to be debated and reformed, Goebbels treated them as scripts to be imposed and rehearsed. The result was not education for judgment but conditioning for obedience. [9].

Viewed through Protagoras and the Sophists, Goebbels shows how potent—and perilous—rhetoric becomes when the ethical brakes are removed. The Sophists treated persuasion as a civic art and trained citizens in antilogikē—arguing both sides—to improve public judgment. Goebbels kept the insight that speech shapes the city, but replaced plural contest with a single, state-owned narrative.

Where Protagoras saw laws and justice as human conventions to be debated and reformed, Goebbels treated them as scripts to be imposed and endlessly rehearsed. The result was not education for judgment but conditioning for obedience. [9].

Lessons from Goebbels' Propaganda
Three lessons follow. First, propaganda that saturates all media can change not only what people think but how they think—narrowing attention to sanctioned contrasts and rehearsed emotions. Second, repetition is not merely a tactic; at scale it becomes a social environment in which dissent sounds implausible before it can be argued. Third, ethics cannot be an afterthought. Sophistic technique requires Sophistic responsibility: to teach citizens how to argue and decide, not how to conform and obey. Goebbels shows the abyss that opens when technique is severed from truth. [4][6].

Three cautions follow. First, saturation propaganda can alter not just opinions but the habits of attention— narrowing thought to preapproved oppositions and rehearsed emotions. Second, repetition at scale becomes an environment; in such a soundscape, dissent sounds implausible before arguments are even offered. Third, technique without ethics is dangerous. Sophistic skill

37

demands Sophistic responsibility: the task is to form citizens able to argue and decide, not to drill them to conform. Goebbels marks the abyss that opens when technique is severed from truth. [4][6].

From Nazi Germany to Cold War Propaganda
The Cold War that followed World War II turned propaganda into a permanent feature of global politics. Democracies and dictatorships alike built media systems to advance narratives, win allies, and demoralize opponents. The next chapter considers how competing "truths" confronted each other across the Iron Curtain—and asks whether Sophistic methods can serve public reason when two rival worlds each claim to be the measure of all things.

In the postwar world, propaganda became a standing feature of international life. Democracies and dictatorships alike built media systems to seed narratives, attract allies, and sap enemy morale. The next chapter looks at the Cold War contest of "truths" across the Iron Curtain—and asks whether Sophistic methods can be used for public reason when rival orders each claim to be the measure of all things.

Endnotes
[1] Peter Longerich, *Goebbels: A Biography* (Random House, 2015), esp. chs. 7–10 on the building of the propaganda ministry and media coordination.

[2] Ian Kershaw, *The "Hitler Myth": Image and Reality in the Third Reich* (Oxford University Press, 1987), on orchestrated consensus, plebiscites, and the leader cult.

[3] Jeffrey Herf, *The Jewish Enemy: Nazi Propaganda during World War II and the Holocaust* (Harvard University Press, 2006), on enemy construction and wartime narratives.

[4] David Welch, *The Third Reich: Politics and Propaganda*, 2nd ed. (Routledge, 2002), on techniques, rallies, radio, and the ethics of propaganda.

[5] Adolf Hitler, *Mein Kampf*, trans. Ralph Manheim (Houghton Mifflin, 1971), on the need for simple, repeated points in mass persuasion.

[6] Eric Rentschler, *The Ministry of Illusion: Nazi Cinema and Its Afterlife* (Harvard University Press, 1996), on film as immersive propaganda.

[7] Richard J. Evans, *The Third Reich in Power, 1933–1939* (Penguin, 2005), on Gleichschaltung, book burnings, and the cultural climate.

[8] Klaus Kreimeier, *The Ufa Story: A History of Germany's Greatest Film Company, 1918–1945* (University of California Press, 1999), on industry control and spectacle.

[9] G. B. Kerferd, *The Sophistic Movement* (Cambridge University Press, 1981), background on Sophistic methods and civic aims.

[Volksempfänger] By 1939, approximately 12.5 million Volksempfänger radios had been sold, making Hitler's broadcasts accessible to most German households

Author's Commentary

As I look back on the first six chapters, I feel it is important to pause for a moment on Protagoras and the Sophists. I do not believe that Protagoras wrote with ill intent. Like other philosophers, he spoke and wrote from his own perspective and experience, sincerely convinced of the truth of what he taught. I know of no philosopher who set out to cause harm, and I do not believe Protagoras would have seen danger in his own words.

And yet, history shows that his approach — when taken up by others — carried risks. By placing persuasion above truth and treating laws and justice as human conventions, Sophistic philosophy opened the door for rhetoric to be used as a tool of power rather than a guide for wisdom. Plato and Aristotle recognized this danger in their own time. They saw that if truth could be reduced to opinion, then the strongest voice, not the best argument, would prevail.

From my perspective, little good came from Sophism for its followers. The legacy it left behind shows how easily rhetoric, detached from ethics, can become destructive. At the same time, I hesitate to make my commentary wholly negative. Protagoras did believe in the power of speech and in the ability of human beings to shape society through dialogue. His faith in rhetoric, to shape society through dialogue. His faith in rhetoric, though flawed, reflected a conviction that citizens could engage with one another and influence the life of their community.

That, I think, is the tension we must carry forward: the recognition that even philosophies born in sincerity can yield outcomes that do not match their author's intentions. Protagoras believed in his words, and for that, he deserves a measure of respect. But the consequences of Sophism also remind us that ideas, once set loose, can shape the world in ways a philosopher never imagined

Chapter 7

The Cold War and Competing Truths

The New Battlefield: Ideas and Narratives
Through a Sophistic lens, the Cold War shows how
communities make truth by instruction and practice.
Protagoras' famous thesis—often summarized as "man
is the measure"—locates judgment within human
perception and civic training. In this struggle, each
superpower sought to become the very measure by
which events were interpreted, teaching audiences how
to see prosperity, justice, and fear through its own
frame [17].

After 1945, the struggle between the United States and
the Soviet Union extended beyond armies and treaties
into the realm of communication itself. Competing
broadcasts, newspapers, films, along with exhibitions,
became the instruments of influence, each side
attempting to showcase its system as the source of truth
while dismissing the other as a machine of falsehoods.
The heart of the conflict was not confined to geography
but to molding beliefs about freedom, justice,
prosperity, and the future course of human society.

American Strategies: Democracy and Free Information

The United States framed itself as the defender of an open society where a free press and open debate allowed truth to surface. Agencies such as the United States Information Agency (USIA, 1953–1999) coordinated cultural programs, libraries, speaker tours, pamphlets, and films abroad. Broadcasting reached behind the Iron Curtain through Voice of America (begun 1942), Radio Free Europe, and Radio Liberty—offering news bulletins, interviews, and cultural programming that contrasted Western pluralism with communist control.

Sophists taught that persuasion depends not only on what is asserted but on what is strategically omitted. American public diplomacy claimed allegiance to factual reporting, yet it curated emphases—foregrounding civil society, markets, and cultural openness while underemphasizing episodes that complicated the narrative. The technique mirrors a classical rhetorical choice: select the premises that help a jury see the case your way, while remaining within the bounds of plausibility.

Book programs, translated and distributed literature; jazz tours and art exhibits presented American creativity as a sign of liberty. These efforts rested on a claim: that accurate information and free exchange would prove persuasive on their own. Yet American messaging also engaged in selective framing—highlighting prosperity and civil rights progress while muting racial violence, political repression during the Red Scare, or covert actions by U.S. intelligence services. The result was a rhetoric that aimed to be truthful but was still strategic.

Soviet Strategies: Ideology and Control
Protagoras held that any logos invites a counter-logos. Soviet information practice institutionalized this 'antilogos' posture—reframing Western claims as exploitation, decadence, or imperialism while narrating socialism as historical necessity. The contest did not simply trade facts; it paired facts with framing, proving that control over interpretive context can rival control over data [18].

The Soviet Union portrayed itself as the spearhead of history, offering socialism as a corrective to capitalism's inequalities and colonial domination. Its state press—led by Pravda and Izvestia, alongside Moscow radio and a tightly managed film sector, delivered a unified story of progress under Communist Party rule.

Editorial control, censorship, and cultural unions ensured that books, cinema, and television all echoed the same official themes. Crises in the West, economic downturns, racial conflict, or foreign wars, were spotlighted as proof of capitalism's weakness, while internal dissent was portrayed as treachery or manipulation by outsiders.

The Battle for the Global South

Like itinerant Sophists adapting arguments to each polis, both superpowers localized their appeals. Aid, education, and media were cast in vocabularies attuned to anti-colonial dignity, industrial modernization, or social equity. Audiences were not passive; leaders and publics interpreted offers through their own needs, showing that persuasion is always contextual, never universal.

Newly decolonized nations in Asia, Africa, and Latin America were the decisive audience of the era. The United States promoted development aid, technical assistance, and consumer abundance as the fruits of market democracy, while the Soviet Union supported anti-colonial movements, offered educational exchanges, and advertised rapid industrialization as a path to dignity and independence.

Both sides built cultural centers, sent touring orchestras and dance companies, and competed at trade fairs. Films and newsreels carried contrasting images of modern life. In many places, local leaders blended, resisted, or played off both narratives to pursue their own agendas, demonstrating that audiences were not passive consumers of propaganda but active interpreters with their own priorities.

Technology, Reach, and the Stagecraft of Credibility
Delivery mattered as much as content. Classical Sophists prized voice, timing, and spectacle; Cold War actors translated these into radio cadence, televised set-pieces, and traveling exhibitions. The 'Kitchen Debate' and Olympic ceremonies functioned like civic performances: they did not merely tell; they showed—anchoring belief through visible, memorable form [18].

Radio remained the most flexible tool. Western broadcasters used local languages, featured defectors and intellectuals, and carried uncensored news into Eastern Europe; Soviet authorities tried to jam these signals (intensively from the late 1940s into the early 1960s, and again in later crises), with varying success.

Television magnified the contest by pairing pictures with narrative: Soviet parades, space triumphs, and industrial showcases versus American suburbs, supermarkets, and civil rights marches. Cultural exchanges, book fairs, and traveling exhibitions became stages on which each system tried to demonstrate everyday credibility, nowhere more visibly than the American National Exhibition in Moscow (1959) and the "Kitchen Debate." Even sporting events and the

Olympic Games served as proofs of national vigor, discipline, and moral standing. The Cold War taught governments to treat attention as a scarce resource and credibility as a strategic asset.

Ethical Tensions in Democratic Persuasion
Plato charged that Sophistic rhetoric risks victory without truth. Democratic policymakers faced the allied dilemma: how to persuade globally without corroding the very norms—openness, contestation, accountable facts—that legitimize persuasion at home. The ethical task is to reconcile strategic communication with standards of evidence that citizens can audit [19].

Democratic states repeatedly wrestled with a dilemma: how could a society that prizes open debate defend the use of state-sponsored persuasion? Policymakers tried to distinguish between providing reliable information and engaging in outright manipulation, maintaining that democratic communication should remain factual, even if it was strategically selective.

A Sophistic Lens on the Cold War: Influence and Scale
Seen through the lens of Protagoras and fellow Sophists, the Cold War functioned as a worldwide demonstration of argument in opposition, with each side advancing its claims as the standard of truth while branding the rival's story as falsehood.

The Sophists taught that persuasion itself helps shape civic life, and in this conflict the superpowers expanded that principle to an unprecedented global scale. Protagoras emphasized that law and justice are grounded in human practice and instruction; the Cold War reworked this idea into bureaucracies, propaganda agencies, and international broadcasting networks.

Case Glimpses: Uprisings, Missiles, and Space

In Protagorean terms, these flashpoints reveal that civic 'truth' is forged where competing arguments meet. The same Hungarian or Czechoslovak scenes could be narrated as liberation or subversion; the Cuban crisis as restraint or brinkmanship. Narratives did not replace reality, but they organized perception—guiding which facts mattered and how they cohered.

Critical moments showed how narratives influenced public opinion. In Hungary (1956) and Czechoslovakia (1968), Western news emphasized grassroots appeals for liberty, while Soviet media characterized the same events as hostile counterrevolutions. The Cuban Missile Crisis likewise became a contest of images and words: both governments sought to steady allies and warn adversaries through televised addresses, circulated photographs, and carefully timed leaks.

At the United Nations on October 25, 1962, U.S. Ambassador Adlai Stevenson famously displayed aerial reconnaissance to dispute Moscow's claims. The space race carried similar weight in shaping perception— Sputnik's launch in 1957 startled Western audiences and bolstered Soviet prestige, while the 1969 moon landing was celebrated as proof of American ingenuity and strength. None of these episodes were decided by propaganda alone, yet the way they were narrated strongly influenced how people understood, feared, and remembered them.

What Endured After 1991
The end of the Soviet Union did not end competition over narratives. Instead, techniques developed during the Cold War migrated into new institutions and technologies. International broadcasters continued under revised mandates; public diplomacy rebranded but persisted. Commercial news networks, NGOs, and multinational corporations joined states as shapers of perception. The habits learned then, staging credibility, managing attention, and pairing values with visible proof—became part of the modern information environment. The line between domestic political messaging and foreign propaganda also thinned as global media flows ignored borders.

Lessons and Responsibilities
The Sophistic insight that persuasion structures public life stands confirmed by the Cold War; Plato's warning that rhetoric needs ethical discipline is equally

confirmed. Modern democracies must therefore pair persuasive capacity with transparent warrants—sources, methods, and evidence trails—so that citizens can test claims rather than merely consume them.

Three conclusions follow from this history. First, information can be wielded like infrastructure: it carries values, priorities, and identities into daily life. Second, competing truths thrive when audiences cannot test claims against transparent evidence; openness matters not only for liberty but for epistemic reliability. Third, persuasion is not neutral. Its power makes ethical discipline necessary, including clarity about sources, methods, and the difference between debate and manipulation. These are classical concerns reborn for a mass-media age.

Bridge to Chapter 8
The next chapter turns to postmodern accounts of truth and power. Thinkers like Michel Foucault and Richard Rorty questioned whether truth stands apart from the discourses and communities that sustain it. Their arguments echo Protagoras in new vocabulary and sharpen the challenge raised by the Cold War: when many voices claim to be the measure, how should citizens judge?

Endnotes

[1] Arch Puddington, *Broadcasting Freedom: The Cold War Triumph of Radio Free Europe and Radio Liberty* (University Press of Kentucky, 2000).

[2] Nicholas J. Cull, *The Cold War and the United States Information Agency: American Propaganda and Public Diplomacy, 1945–1989* (Cambridge University Press, 2008).

[3] Yale Richmond, *Cultural Exchange and the Cold War: Raising the Iron Curtain* (Pennsylvania State University Press, 2003).

[4] Kristin Roth-Ey, *Moscow Prime Time: How the Soviet Union Built the Media Empire that Lost the Cultural Cold War* (Cornell University Press, 2011).

[5] David Welch, *Propaganda: Power and Persuasion* (The British Library, 2013), esp. Cold War chapters.

[6] Tony Shaw, *Hollywood's Cold War* (Edinburgh University Press, 2007).

[7] Hope M. Harrison, *Driving the Soviets up the Wall: Soviet–East German Relations, 1953–1961* (Princeton University Press, 2003).

[8] Odd Arne Westad, *The Global Cold War: Third World Interventions and the Making of Our Times* (Cambridge University Press, 2005).

[9] Alan L. Heil Jr., *Voice of America: A History* (Columbia University Press, 2003).

[10] Thomas C. Wolfe, *Governing Soviet Journalism: The Press and the Socialist Person after Stalin* (Indiana University Press, 2005).

[11] U.S. National Archives, "If You Can't Take the Heat…," on the 1959 American National Exhibition and the 'Kitchen Debate' (blog, July 26, 2012).

[12] Office of the Historian, U.S. Department of State, *Foreign Relations of the United States* (various vols.), including documentation on USIA's 1953 creation and mission separation from educational exchanges.

[13] NASA, "Sputnik and the Dawn of the Space Age," NASA History Program Office (accessed Sept. 26, 2025).

[14] Library of Congress, "[Adlai Stevenson describes location of missile sites in Cuba using aerial photographs…]" photo record (1962).

[15] Woodrow Wilson International Center for Scholars, *Cold War International History Project*, "Role of Radio Free Europe in the Hungarian Revolution of 1956" (Working Paper/Occasional Paper).

[16] *Foreign Relations of the United States*, 1964–1968, Vol. XIV, "Soviet Union," docs on Soviet jamming of Western broadcasts.

[17] Plato, *Theaetetus*, in *Plato: Complete Works*, ed. John M. Cooper, trans. M. J. Levett (rev. Myles Burnyeat) (Hackett, 1997), 151e–152a (the "man is the measure" doctrine).
[18] Rosamond Kent Sprague, ed., *The Older Sophists* (Hackett, 2001), selections on antilogos and rhetorical method.
[19] Plato, *Gorgias*, in *Plato: Complete Works*, trans. Donald J. Zeyl (Hackett, 1997), esp. 454c–465e (Plato's critique of rhetoric and sophistry).

[20] Gorgias, *Encomium of Helen*, in Rosamond Kent Sprague, ed., *The Older Sophists* (Hackett, 2001), esp. sections 8–14 on the enchanting power of logos

Chapter 8

Postmodernism and Power

Re-centering the Measure: Protagoras as the Frame

This book treats truth and persuasion through Protagoras and the Sophists. Here we keep that lens. Protagoras' claim—"man is the measure"—means that what counts as true is judged from inside human life: by persons, practices, and cities. The question for this chapter is simple: How do two modern currents—Foucault and Rorty—restate that Sophistic insight, and where do they risk the very dangers Plato warned about?

From Dissoi Logoi to "Regimes of Truth" (Foucault)

The Sophists trained citizens in antilogikē—double arguments—so a city could weigh rival claims. Michel Foucault extends that civic insight into modern institutions.

He argues that what a society accepts as "true" is organized by power/knowledge: courts, schools, clinics, laboratories, and media form regimes of truth that certify who may speak, what counts as evidence, and which procedures settle disputes. In Sophistic terms, he is saying that the "measure" is set by public practices, not by a view from nowhere.

Discipline, Biopower, and the New Civic Craft

Classical Athens commonly used public speeches and laws to mold their citizens. Modern states employ discipline by shaping habits and behaviors through institutions such as schools, prisons, military barracks, and hospitals.

They also exercise a form of biopower by regulating populations through statistical monitoring, systems of surveillance, and public health standards. This mode of control works through administrative tools—schedules, record-keeping, and procedural rules—that classify individuals and steer their decisions. The Sophists taught citizens to argue; the modern order often pre-structures the argument before anyone speaks.

Discourse and the Expert

For Foucault, a discourse is a rule-bound way of seeing—medical, legal, scientific, that frames problems and authorizes experts. A discourse does not only name facts; it makes certain facts actionable. That is a Protagorean move: truth shows up inside a shared craft. The risk is also Sophistic: the craft can serve power rather than judgment if counter-speech is muted.

Genealogy: How "Truths" Become Normal

Foucault's genealogy asks how familiar "truths" took shape, what struggles they resolved, whom they silenced, but also, which paths they closed. This is not "anything goes." It is a civic caution: before we obey a norm, ask who benefits and who is missing. Here, the Sophistic impulse to test both sides meets a historian's file-work.

Rorty and the Civic Game of Justification

Richard Rorty shifts the focus from representation to justification. He rejects the picture of the mind as a mirror copying reality. In practice, we trade reasons with our peers and settle on what we can responsibly defend to one another. "Truth," on this view, is not a magic stamp that ends debate; it is a word we use when a claim has survived serious criticism within a community. That is recognizably Sophistic: what holds in a city is what we can argue for and live with together.

Solidarity over Foundations

Rorty urges solidarity—wider sympathy, more inclusive conversation—over the hunt for foundations. Vocabularies are tools we inherit and revise; progress looks like reducing cruelty and widening the circle of reasons. The Sophistic echo is clear: teach citizens to argue well, translate across groups, and accept that public truth is worked out, not discovered by oracle.

Where the Two Meet—and Where They Part

Foucault and Rorty both hold on to Protagoras's central claim that truth is measured within the scope of human practice rather than against some transcendent standard. In this sense, both resist the illusion that experts can speak from a neutral, universal standpoint, a "view from nowhere." Yet they diverge in what they see as the chief danger and in the remedies they propose.

Foucault emphasizes how truth practices can conceal systems of power and domination, calling for critical exposure of the ways authority embeds itself in knowledge. Rorty, by contrast, is less concerned with hidden coercion than with the rigidity of "final vocabularies" that stifle conversation. His remedy is not exposure but continual redescription, keeping dialogue open and vocabularies flexible.

Plato's Rejoinder, Re-engaged

Plato warned that unmoored persuasion becomes flattery and that radical relativism risks self-refutation. Our answer, still within the Sophistic frame, is to add guardrails to civic craft: transparency of methods, rights of dissent, cross-examination, and correction. These are institutional ways to honor Protagoras (truth is humanly measured) without surrendering to mere performance. Chapters 1–3 posed this tension; here we sharpen it for modern life.

Ethical Duties Inside Practice

If truth lives inside practice, ethics must, too. Three duties follow: 1) Transparency—disclose data, methods, and interests so citizens can test claims. 2) Contestability—protect spaces where double arguments are safe and expected. 3) Responsibility—use critique to widen inclusion, not only to unmask. In short, Sophistic technique requires Sophistic ethics.

What Changes in the Platform Era (Preview)

In Athens, juries and assemblies set the stage for dissoi logoi. Today, platform design and attention metrics set the stage. Algorithms pick salience; interfaces shape what looks credible; speed rewards style. The Sophistic lesson still applies: if the measure is public practice, then engineering choices are ethical choices about truth's conditions.

Bridge to Chapter 9

Chapter 9 turns from theory to the infrastructures that now teach publics how to see: 24-hour news, feeds, recommender systems, and influencer markets. We will ask how to build room for double arguments into those systems so that persuasion remains a civic craft rather than an engine of domination.

Endnotes

1. Michel Foucault, "Truth and Power," in Power/Knowledge: Selected Interviews and Other

Writings, 1972–1977, ed. Colin Gordon (Pantheon, 1980); Michel Foucault, The Archaeology of Knowledge (Routledge, 2002 [1969]).

2. Michel Foucault, Discipline and Punish: The Birth of the Prison (Vintage, 1995 [1975]); Michel Foucault, The History of Sexuality, Vol. 1 (Vintage, 1990 [1976]).

3. Hubert L. Dreyfus and Paul Rabinow, Michel Foucault: Beyond Structuralism and Hermeneutics, 2nd ed. (University of Chicago Press, 1983); Gary Gutting, Foucault: A Very Short Introduction (Oxford University Press, 2005).

4. Richard Rorty, Philosophy and the Mirror of Nature (Princeton University Press, 1979); Objectivity, Relativism, and Truth (Cambridge University Press, 1991).

5. Richard Rorty, Contingency, Irony, and Solidarity (Cambridge University Press, 1989).

6. Richard Rorty, Truth and Progress: Philosophical Papers, Vol. 3 (Cambridge University Press, 1998)

Chapter 9
Media in the 21st Century

Introduction: From the Agora to the Algorithm
In ancient Athens, persuasion was central to civic life.
Citizens argued their cases in assemblies and courts,
often without lawyers. Teachers like Protagoras showed
that truth was not a divine gift but a human practice.
His famous claim, "Man is the measure of all things,"
meant that people must judge truth by testing claims
through speech and debate.

Today, the debate no longer happens in stone plazas but
on glowing screens. The modern public square is made
of 24-hour news cycles, social-media feeds, and
recommendation systems that quietly decide what we
see. Instead of listening to orators in person, billions of
people scroll through headlines, videos, and posts each
day.

The pattern is familiar: what persuades people often
becomes what they accept as true. Speaking well is still
a civic skill, though the audience is now global.
Journalists, commentators, and influencers shape how
events are understood. They may not call themselves
philosophers, but their words still guide public
judgment.

There is, however, a new difference. In Athens, persuasion was delivered face to face. Now, attention is captured by platforms that profit from clicks, views, and likes. Popularity is measured in numbers, and those numbers decide which voices are heard.

The speed of persuasion has also changed. Speeches in the past could last hours. Today, persuasion happens in seconds through headlines, images, and viral posts that cross the globe instantly. This raises a new question: can truth survive when persuasion is fast, monetized, and automated?

Protagoras reminds us that truth has always been shaped by human practice, not by a perfect, outside standard. If persuasion is the measure, then the way the media is designed is an ethical choice. This chapter looks at how news networks, social-media algorithms, echo chambers, influencers, and "fake news" shape truth today—and what rules might help keep persuasion honest.

Editorials as Persuasive Aftershocks

When news coverage leans heavily toward one side of a debate, the effect rarely ends with the report itself. Modern networks and digital outlets often follow their slanted presentation with editorials or commentary that reinforce the same framing. What begins as selective reporting is then amplified by authoritative opinion, shaping how audiences interpret the facts.

From a Sophistic standpoint, this two-step process—first setting the angle, then endorsing it—mirrors the rhetorical strategies of ancient teachers. Protagoras accepted that persuasion is woven into all speech, but he also warned that stronger arguments must be tested against weaker ones. When media organizations build a chain of persuasion where reporting flows seamlessly into editorials, the audience risks mistaking confirmation for balance.

For Protagoras, this would not negate truth but reveal how fragile it is when citizens fail to practice dissoi logoi. The Sophists understood that persuasion often comes in layers: a speech, followed by interpretation, followed by repetition. Modern editorials act as these persuasive aftershocks, guiding perception until opinion feels like fact. The ethical danger arises when citizens no longer recognize the shift, treating commentary as the natural continuation of truth.

Plato would have viewed this pattern as especially dangerous, since persuasion here serves attention and influence rather than careful judgment. In this sense, the blending of news and editorial content embodies both the Sophistic insight—that truth is always shaped in practice—and Plato's warning—that persuasion without restraint can dissolve judgment into spectacle.

24-Hour News as Modern Rhetoric

The rise of 24-hour cable news in the late 20th century changed how persuasion worked. CNN's launch in 1980 proved that news could run without pause, instead of arriving once a day in print or evening broadcasts [1]. The effect was not just more coverage. It created a permanent stage for persuasion.

Like ancient orators, modern networks rely on style and delivery. They turn routine events into urgent stories, and anchors frame facts in ways that invite agreement, alarm, or anger. Emotional images, repeating themes, and simplified contrasts are tools straight from the old rhetorical playbook.

But when every story is labeled "breaking news," the line between important and trivial blurs. What counts as significant becomes what can be narrated quickly. Here, Protagoras seems right: truth is shaped by how events appear and how people respond.

Plato's warning also applies. If persuasion is driven by ratings instead of knowledge, spectacle can replace wisdom. Audiences reward networks with attention, and advertisers reward them with money. Journalism risks sliding into entertainment.

Still, not all outcomes are negative. Protagoras admitted that expertise can sharpen judgment. Many journalists today remain committed to careful verification and context. Yet they must compete in an attention economy that constantly pushes toward the dramatic.

The danger is not only false information but shallow understanding. A public that reacts quickly but does not reflect deeply becomes skilled at consuming updates but weak at forming judgment.

For Protagoras, then, editorialized news would not be a violation of truth but a reminder of how truth emerges. He would accept that every report is already an act of persuasion, shaped by choices of language and context.

What matters is whether the audience is prepared to meet persuasion with skill. In this way, Protagoras would find the media's blending of fact and opinion acceptable—not because it guarantees truth, but because it reflects the human practice through which truth must always be discovered.

This does not mean that all framings are equal. Protagoras believed that some judgments are better than others, and that training in argument and comparison could improve them. He would likely insist that citizens, when faced with editorialized news, must apply the discipline of dissoi logoi—hearing multiple sides, weighing the differences, and forming reasoned conclusions. If the public mistakes commentary for unfiltered fact, it is not because persuasion has failed, but because judgment has grown weak.

Protagoras's famous claim, "Man is the measure of all things," makes clear that truth is never free of context. Facts do not speak for themselves; they are weighed, framed, and understood by people in practice. When the media selects certain images, highlights particular voices, or stresses one angle over another, it is not distorting an otherwise pure reality. It is performing the act of persuasion that has always been central to civic judgment.

Modern media often blurs the line between fact and commentary. News is presented not only as a list of events but as a story shaped by tone, emphasis, and interpretation. Critics argue this practice misleads the public, taking information out of context and turning reports into editorials disguised as facts. From a Sophistic perspective, however, such blending is not a betrayal of truth but part of how truth has always been formed in public life.

Protagoras on Media Blending Fact and Opinion
Modern news often mixes reporting with opinion. Stories are shaped not only by facts but also by tone, choice of images, and the way information is arranged. Critics warn that this can mislead the public by presenting commentary as fact. Yet from a Sophistic point of view, this blending is not a failure but a reflection of how truth has always been shaped through human judgment.

Protagoras's idea that "man is the measure of all things" means that truth always comes through context. Facts do not carry meaning on their own—they gain weight only when people interpret and respond to them. When the media highlights certain details or voices, it is not twisting a perfect reality but practicing persuasion, which has always been central to civic life.

Still, not every version of a story is equally strong. Protagoras believed that training in argument could help people tell stronger judgments from weaker ones. He would likely say that when audiences meet opinionated reporting, their task is to test it against other views. If citizens accept commentary as fact without questioning it, the problem lies not only with the speaker but with the listener's failure to deliberate.

From this view, editorialized reporting is not a break from truth but a reminder of its process. Every report is already shaped by language and perspective. What matters is whether the public meets persuasion with skill and reflection. Protagoras would likely accept this blending—not as a guarantee of truth, but as part of the human practice through which truth is discovered.

Social-Media Algorithms and Dissoi Logoi

The Sophists taught dissoi logoi—arguing both sides— to strengthen judgment. Digital platforms could, in theory, continue this practice by exposing people to many views. In practice, algorithmic design and user choices often do the opposite.

Research shows that both ranking systems and personal habits limit exposure to opposing views [3–4]. People usually click on content that confirms what they already believe, and algorithms learn to supply more of it. Profit and comfort align.

This narrows persuasion into private streams. Where Protagoras imagined citizens facing open contest, algorithms sort people into separate realities. Shared debate turns into parallel conversations.

The risk is extreme relativism: "man is the measure" becomes "my feed is the measure." Communities that rarely meet serious counterarguments lose the skill of weighing reasons. The practice of dissoi logoi fades away.

Design matters. Algorithms built to maximize clicks and watch time usually favor novelty, emotion, and identity-based content over balance or context [8]. If persuasion shapes truth, then designing these systems is a civic responsibility, not just a technical task.

Reform is possible. Platforms can adjust ranking signals, give users more control, and slow the rapid spread of unverified claims. These steps would restore a modern form of dissoi logoi—ensuring persuasive speech meets credible counter-speech.

Echo Chambers, Influencers, and the New Sophists

Critics once accused the Sophists of selling persuasion for profit. Today's influencer economy brings this charge back in digital form. Persuasion is a business, and trust is traded for sponsorships, affiliate deals, and brand contracts—activities that U.S. law requires to be disclosed under the FTC's Endorsement Guides [5].

Influence relies on ethos—authenticity, relatability, aspiration. Many creators give ordinary people a public voice, bypassing traditional gatekeepers. This can expand democracy. Yet the same system often rewards outrage or spectacle over balance, encouraging persuasion that entertains more than it educates.

Echo chambers add to the challenge. Communities form around shared identity, and dissent can carry social costs. Inside these spaces, truth is reinforced through repetition rather than debate.

Still, not all persuasion here is shallow. Some creators use their reach for education, reform, or investigation. They continue the Sophistic aim of shaping civic understanding. The real question is whether platform incentives allow this kind of work to survive at scale.

Plato's critique still matters: persuasion that pleases without improving weakens society. Guardrails such as disclosure rules, limits on hidden amplification, and promotion of informative content can align influence with judgment.

The new Sophists, then, are not villains or saviors by nature. Their value depends on the structures that shape their speech.

"Fake News" and Relativism

Few issues show the struggle over truth more sharply than what people call "fake news." The term is used both for intentional lies and as a weapon to dismiss reports people dislike. This double use fuels relativism, where each group accepts its own version of truth and rejects others.

Research shows why this is so persistent. On Twitter (now X), false stories were found to spread faster and farther than accurate ones, even when bots were not counted [2]. Newness and emotional punch make lies more likely to travel [6].

Digital tools make the problem worse. Edited images, artificial voices, and deep-fake videos make it cheap to create false stories but costly to disprove them [7]. Once a false claim spreads, later corrections rarely catch up—the original message usually runs ahead, leaving truth lagging behind.

This feeds cynicism. Some people conclude that "everything is spin," and give up on judgment altogether. Protagoras would not accept this. He argued that while all truth is shaped by people, some judgments are better than others. Expertise and practice can still refine how we tell truth from falsehood.

The task, then, is twofold: protect open debate while also strengthening shared standards of evidence. Fact-checking, source transparency, and civic education play this role. They cannot erase relativism, but they can guide it so that disagreement sharpens judgment instead of destroying trust.

Provenance matters as well. Clear source labels, visible corrections, and update logs help the public tell apart simple mistakes from deliberate deception. These practices cannot create absolute certainty, but they rebuild trust by making the process of verification open and visible.

Guardrails for Modern Civic Practice
If truth is shaped within human practice, then media design carries ethical responsibility. Ancient Athens used institutions—open assemblies, cross-examinations, rights of speech—to hold persuasion accountable. Today's systems need similar guardrails of transparency, contestability, and responsibility.

Transparency means citizens should know how information is ranked and shown. Hidden systems make persuasion invisible and more open to manipulation.

Contestability protects dissoi logoi. Claims must be open to challenge, and ranking systems should highlight—not hide—responsible disagreement. Systems that bury opposing views undercut civic judgment.

Responsibility completes the triad. Journalists, creators, and platform engineers shape not only what is said but also how judgment is formed. Professional standards, such as the Society of Professional Journalists' Code—seek truth, minimize harm, act independently, and remain accountable—are anchors in today's attention economy [6].

History offers warnings. Propaganda without ethics reduces rhetoric to domination. Powerful institutions can silently decide what counts as truth. Liberal pragmatists remind us that solidarity, not absolute certainty, sustains public reason. Together, these lessons show that persuasion needs structure to serve the common good.

Guardrails, then, are not outside of persuasion but part of it. Citizens must be trained to argue well, to see multiple sides, and to hold institutions accountable. Without such measures, truth risks dissolving into noise.

Conclusion: Protagoras in the Platform Era

From the agora to the algorithm, persuasion has remained central to civic life. Protagoras taught that truth depends on human practice. The Sophists showed that rhetoric can uplift or corrupt. Plato warned that persuasion without guidance turns into flattery. All three lessons remain relevant today.

Twenty-four-hour news and partisan media reveal the power of style. Algorithms show how hidden systems can steer judgment. Influencers and echo chambers carry both the promise and the danger of democratic speech. "Fake news" exposes the threat of relativism, while ethical guardrails show the need for structure.

The challenge today is scale. Athens trained thousands; platforms shape billions. Athenian jurors heard arguments directly; modern audiences rely on invisible systems. The risks are greater, but so are the chances for renewal if systems are designed to broaden, not narrow, the exchange of reasons.

Taking Protagoras seriously means accepting that truth will always come from human practice. Taking Plato seriously means demanding that persuasion serve more than attention. The task is not to abolish rhetoric but to guide it—to create institutions and technologies that make truth stronger than falsehood. That is the civic craft of the twenty-first century.

Endnotes

[1] "CNN | History, Programs, & Facts," Encyclopaedia Britannica, last updated September 18, 2025. https://www.britannica.com/money/CNN.

[2] Soroush Vosoughi, Deb Roy, and Sinan Aral, "The Spread of True and False News Online," Science 359, no. 6380 (2018): 1146–1151. https://www.science.org/doi/10.1126/science.aap9559.

[3] Eytan Bakshy, Solomon Messing, and Lada A. Adamic, "Exposure to Ideologically Diverse News and Opinion on Facebook," Science 348, no. 6239 (2015): 1130–1132. https://isps.yale.edu/sites/default/files/files/Exposure%20to%20Ideologically%20Diverse%20News%20and%20Opinion%20on%20Facebook.pdf.

[4] Seth Flaxman, Sharad Goel, and Justin M. Rao, "Filter Bubbles, Echo Chambers, and Online News Consumption," Public Opinion Quarterly 80, S1 (2016): 298–320. https://academic.oup.com/poq/article/80/S1/298/2223402.

[5] Federal Trade Commission, "Disclosures 101 for Social Media Influencers," November 2019. https://www.ftc.gov/business-

guidance/resources/disclosures-101-social-media-influencers.

[6] Society of Professional Journalists, "SPJ Code of Ethics," 2014. https://www.spj.org/spj-code-of-ethics/ (PDF: https://www.spj.org/pdf/spj-code-of-ethics.pdf).

[7] Robert Chesney and Danielle Citron, "Deep Fakes: A Looming Challenge for Privacy, Democracy, and National Security," California Law Review 107 (2019): 1753–1819. https://www.californialawreview.org/print/deep-fakes-a-looming-challenge-for-privacy-democracy-and-national-security.

Taking Protagoras seriously means accepting that truth will always come from human practice. Taking Plato seriously means insisting that persuasion must rise above applause, aiming instead at truth and the common good

Chapter 10

Elections and the Persuasive State

Introduction: Democracy as a Contest of Persuasion

Elections transform persuasion into a kind of public truth. Just as citizens in ancient Athens relied on the Sophists to learn courtroom and civic argument, today's voters navigate speeches, debates, and campaign stories that shape their judgment. Protagoras's remark that "man is the measure of all things" (Plato, Theaetetus 152a[1]) captures this dynamic: truth in political life depends not on abstract absolutes but on how people receive and interpret arguments.

Plato cautioned that such persuasion could slip into flattery—rhetoric that entertains but does not teach. Aristotle acknowledged its role but insisted it must serve reason and evidence. Their warnings remind us that persuasion in elections can either deepen civic understanding or distort it, depending on how it is used (see Plato, Gorgias[2]; Aristotle, Rhetoric I.1–I.2[3]).

Elections are the modern stage where persuasion becomes public truth. Candidates, parties, and citizens alike enter into a contest of speech that resembles the Athenian assembly of Protagoras's time. In that earlier world, the Sophists trained citizens to use rhetoric not only to defend themselves in court but also to guide the city in matters of law and policy. For them, persuasion was the lifeblood of democracy.

Protagoras's famous phrase—"man is the measure of all things" (Protagoras, reported in Plato, *Theaetetus* 152a^1)—is especially sharp here. In elections, truth is not decided in isolation but by the people who weigh speeches, debates, and narratives. Campaigns do not simply present facts; they frame reality, telling stories that aim to move whole communities.

Plato, however, warned that rhetoric could fall into flattery: it may please without teaching, stir emotions without guiding to wisdom. Aristotle followed by acknowledging rhetoric's place but insisting it must serve reason and truth. Together, their warnings remind us that the persuasive state can educate citizens or deceive them, depending on how rhetoric is used (see Plato, *Gorgias*^2) (see Aristotle, *Rhetoric* I.1–I.2^3).

Section 1 – Campaign Rhetoric and Narrative Management

Campaign rhetoric reduces the vast complexity of political life into stories that ordinary people can grasp and repeat. Slogans, images, and repeated phrases become tools for shaping public judgment. To the Sophists, this was a natural part of civic life. They taught that a common ancient charge—voiced in sources like Aristophanes' *Clouds*^4—was that sophists could "make the weaker argument the stronger." Protagoras himself argued that what seems true to citizens is what becomes true in practice [56]

Narrative management is the organized version of this same art. Modern campaigns coordinate speeches, debates, interviews, and advertisements so that one central storyline dominates attention. This is not unlike the Sophistic technique of teaching students to prepare both sides of a case so they could manage perception. Yet where the Sophists sought to train individuals, modern campaigns aim to train entire electorates in a single narrative.[7]

Plato would caution that such management risks turning rhetoric into spectacle. By focusing only on applause, campaigns may win the crowd while neglecting wisdom. Aristotle would counter that rhetoric can still serve truth if its claims are supported by evidence, character, and logic. In either case, both philosophers saw the danger of persuasion detached from principle (see Plato, *Gorgias*^2) (see Aristotle, *Rhetoric* I.1– I.2^3).

Section 2 – Truth and Lies as Matters of Perception
For Protagoras and the Sophists, truth was never a fixed object waiting to be discovered. Instead, it lived in perception. Protagoras's famous claim that "man is the

measure of all things" makes this clear: what appears true to a person or to a community becomes truth in practice. A statement is not judged by correspondence to some absolute reality, but by how it is received and accepted [8]

This perspective reshapes the meaning of lies as well. If truth is grounded in perception, then a lie is not simply a falsehood but an alternative framing—another attempt to persuade an audience. Lies gain or lose power depending on whether people perceive them as convincing. In this model, the difference between truth and falsehood collapses into the difference between what persuades and what fails to persuade.[910]

The Sophists taught rhetoric precisely as the art of managing these perceptions. By showing how weaker arguments could be made stronger, they revealed that civic truth is malleable. What the people judge persuasive in the courts, assemblies, or elections is what becomes real for the community. Protagoras would therefore see persuasion not as an enemy of truth but as its very foundation.[11]

Section 3 – Case Studies from Recent Elections

Recent elections across the world illustrate how persuasion shapes outcomes. Campaigns often rely on repetition, identity appeals, and emotional language—methods the Sophists would instantly recognize. In some cases, digital tools have amplified these strategies: slogans spread rapidly online, emotional appeals go viral, and visual clips outweigh detailed arguments.

In the United States, candidates in recent cycles have managed competing narratives by emphasizing simple contrasts: strength vs. weakness, continuity vs. change. In Europe, parties have used rhetoric to frame identity and belonging, shaping debates over immigration and unity. In Latin America, campaign strategies often highlight populist appeals, presenting leaders as voices of the people against elites. Each case is different, but the persuasive methods overlap with ancient Sophistic techniques.

Protagoras might argue that these practices are unavoidable—citizens judge what is most persuasive, and that judgment itself becomes truth for the city. Plato, in contrast, would see the same cases as warnings: when narratives outweigh deliberation, elections risk drifting into flattery. Aristotle would ask whether rhetoric here is tied to evidence and reality or whether it is only performance. The case studies remind us that persuasion is not just a tool; it defines the very conditions of modern democracy.

Section 4 – Non-Partisan Treatment of Persuasion

It is tempting to ask who was right and who was wrong in an election. Yet to remain faithful to the philosophical inquiry, we must look instead at how persuasion worked. Did campaigns frame issues clearly? Did citizens have access to both sides? Were arguments supported by reasons, or were they carried mainly by emotion? These questions mirror the Sophists' method of examining speech as craft rather than judging only by outcome.

Protagoras and his peers would point out that persuasion is an equalizer: anyone trained in rhetoric could, in principle, persuade a crowd. Yet in practice, access to resources—money, media, data—creates unequal conditions. That tension echoes the ancient world, where only those who could afford Sophistic training had the skills to thrive in court or assembly.

Plato's warning is clear here. When persuasion is treated as pure competition, the wealthy or well-connected may overwhelm others with style and spectacle. Aristotle offers balance: rhetoric should remain part of civic life, but it must be guided by fairness, openness, and evidence. A non-partisan analysis keeps the focus not on winners but on whether rhetoric served judgment.

Section 5 – The Ethical Dilemma
A common interpretation of Protagoras's measure doctrine is that civic truth is inseparable from the outcomes of persuasion—what the community accepts through deliberation becomes binding in practice.

Plato's response is less forgiving. He would argue that such thinking lowers truth to mere opinion, leaving the city vulnerable to manipulation. In Gorgias, he compared rhetoric without principle to flattery, warning that it pleases but does not teach. Aristotle sought a middle ground: rhetoric should be taught, but it must be tied to character and evidence. Persuasion, he argued, should point toward reality, not away from it.

The ethical dilemma remains unresolved. Campaigns are rewarded for winning, and sometimes the most effective persuasion is not the most truthful. This tension is the heart of the persuasive state: it cannot avoid rhetoric, but it must guard against rhetoric that abandons truth.

Section 6 – Does Winning Persuasion Matter More Than the Truth?

This final question strikes at the foundation of democratic practice. In elections, persuasion often determines who governs. Yet does that mean persuasion is more important than truth? For Protagoras, the answer may be yes: persuasion defines truth in civic life. For Plato, the answer is a warning: persuasion without truth destroys justice. For Aristotle, the answer is conditional: persuasion matters, but it must remain anchored in reality.

When citizens reward only performance, truth can be overshadowed. But when institutions, education, and civic culture emphasize the testing of claims, persuasion and truth can align. That was the original hope of the Sophists—citizens trained to weigh both sides—and the demand of Plato and Aristotle, who insisted rhetoric must be disciplined by reason.

Thus, whether winning persuasion matters more than truth depends not on rhetoric itself but on how a society chooses to guide it. Elections reveal that choice every time citizens step into the voting booth.

Conclusion: Elections as a Sophistic Arena—With Guardrails

Elections will always be theaters of persuasion. That is not a flaw to be eliminated but a fact to be governed. Protagoras gives us the starting point: truth in public life is measured through speech and judgment.

The Sophists teach the skills citizens need: to hear both sides, to name frames, and to test reasons. Their method scales to modern tools if we choose to scale it through design choices, public education, and clear rules.

Plato is the warning light on the dashboard. When style outruns substance, when cadence replaces checking, and when victory becomes the only virtue, democracy forgets why it speaks at all.

Aristotle is the engineer's guide. Tie persuasion to verifiable claims. Build forums that slow heat and speed light. Reward speakers whose character and evidence hold up under scrutiny.

Recent elections show both sides of the ledger: creative speech that helps citizens see, and deceptive tools that try to keep citizens from seeing. The right response is neither panic nor naïveté, but craft—ethical design and trained judgment.

Does winning persuasion matter more than the truth? It can, if we let the forum decay. It need not, if we rebuild the forum to favor reasons that last longer than a news cycle.

The task is continuous: keep elections as contests of reasoned persuasion rather than competitions of influence. That is how a persuasive state stays a democratic one—by making truth easier to see than the lie that races ahead.

Endnotes

1. Plato, Theaetetus, 152a.

2. Plato, Gorgias.

3. Aristotle, Rhetoric, Book I, chs. 1–2.

4. Aristophanes, Clouds.

5. Kathleen Hall Jamieson, *Packaging the Presidency: A History and Criticism of Presidential Campaign Advertising* (Oxford University Press, 1996).

6. G. B. Kerferd, *The Sophistic Movement* (Cambridge University Press, 1981).

7. Roderick P. Hart, *Campaign Talk: Why Elections Are Good for Us* (Princeton University Press, 2000).

8. Plato, *Theaetetus*, 152a–c; Edward Schiappa, *Protagoras and Logos: A Study in Greek Philosophy and Rhetoric* (University of South Carolina Press, 1991).

9. Barbara Cassin, *Sophistical Practice: Toward a Consistent Relativism* (Fordham University Press, 2014).

10. Thomas M. Robinson, *Contrasting Arguments: An Edition of Dissoi Logoi* (Aris & Phillips, 1979).

11. G. B. Kerferd, *The Sophistic Movement* (Cambridge University Press, 1981

Chapter 11
Ethics of Truth in the Modern Polis

Introduction: Truth in the Contemporary City

Truth in the modern polis does not emerge in isolation. It is mediated by three forces. media, government, and citizens. Each is bound by ethical responsibilities. In the connected age of digital networks and global information, persuasion has become both more powerful and more fragile. Campaigns, headlines, and social movements compete not only for attention but for standing as the voice of truth.

The pressing question is not whether persuasion should exist, but whether it should be restrained by principle. Plato warned that relativism breeds contradiction: when truth is reduced to whatever seems persuasive in the moment, societies risk undermining themselves from within.^2 Aristotle, by contrast, sought balance. admitting rhetoric's place. insisting that persuasion must be tied to evidence, character, and reason.^3

These ancient insights echo sharply in our time, as governments spin narratives, media platforms boost messages, and citizens weigh competing voices. Protagoras's remark that "man is the measure of all things" captures this dynamic in public life, where truth often depends on how people receive it. interpret arguments (Plato, Theaetetus 152a).^1

The ethical challenge for the modern polis is to avoid surrendering to relativism while still preserving open persuasion. Media, government, and citizens must all ask: are our words serving the pursuit of truth, or are they tools of expedience? Without principles, persuasion risks becoming a contradiction that wears down civic trust.

Section 1 – The Ethical Burden of Media

The media today occupies the role once played by the agora in Athens: it is the forum where citizens encounter competing claims and where collective perception is formed. With such power comes a profound ethical duty. News outlets and platforms do not merely describe reality.

They select, frame, and boost certain aspects of it. In this act of framing, they participate directly in shaping civic truth. When media outlets collapse the boundary between reporting and commentary, persuasion turns disguise as fact. Editorials are essential in democratic life, but they must remain clear as opinion. If blurred, they risk guiding citizens under the pretense of neutrality.

The ethical demand here is clarity: facts must be distinguished from the interpretations built around them. Modern technologies have magnified this problem. Algorithms determine which stories are seen and which are buried. A sensational claim can reach millions in minutes, while careful reporting struggles for attention. The pressure for media organizations is to favor what is viral over what is verified.

Yet this pressure contradicts their civic duty. Plato's warning applies: rhetoric that pleases. does not teach undermines wisdom.^2 The ethical burden of media, then, is not only to report but to resist the pull of relativism. To treat all perspectives as equally valid, even when some are clearly false, is to breed conflict. If every claim is given equal weight, the very concept of truth dissolves. Instead, the media must stand as a filter. boosting what can be verified and contextualized, while exposing persuasion that lacks grounding.

A free press is essential, but freedom does not absolve duty. Ethical reporting requires guidance: cross-checking sources, separating evidence from speculation, and resisting the easy lure of sensationalism. This is not censorship but civic integrity. As Aristotle insisted, persuasion must remain tied to character and evidence.^3

In election seasons, the media's choices about coverage and framing can shape what the public takes to be true. Historical studies of campaign communication show how repetition, imagery, and narrative can normalize claims that have weak evidence to support.^4 The point is not to silence persuasion. to make sure it remains accountable to verification.

Section 2 – Government and the Duty of Candor

Government carries a unique ethical burden because it holds the authority to act on behalf of the community. When the government persuades, it does so not as one voice among many but as an institution that directs policy, enforces law, and commands resources.

With such authority, the ethical stakes of persuasion multiply. Political leaders often face the pressure to use rhetoric strategically. to maintain standing, to calm unrest, or to justify policy. Yet persuasion detached from truth becomes dangerous.

Plato warned that rhetoric without principle degenerates into flattery, pleasing the people in the moment. failing to serve justice.^2 Relativism, when adopted by rulers, breeds contradiction: policies may shift with public opinion rather than with reasoned principle, leaving citizens unsure of what is truly binding.

History offers sobering examples: leaders who twisted facts to maintain control often found that conflict undermined their credibility over time. Citizens may be persuaded once, but repeated falsehoods erode trust in institutions. Without trust, even truthful claims are doubted.

This erosion of standing is precisely what Plato feared when persuasion is severed from truth.^2 Aristotle's perspective offers a corrective. He acknowledged that rhetoric is inevitable in governance. He insisted that leaders must appeal to evidence, character, and logical argument.^3 A ruler who speaks with honesty, supports claims with evidence, and demonstrates consistent character strengthens the polis rather than weakens it.

Thus, the ethical duty of government is candor. presenting truth transparently, even when it risks short-term unpopularity. Candor preserves long-term standing. Persuasion guided by expedience may win votes or applause, but persuasion tied to principle sustains justice and trust.

In this sense, the government's duty is not simply to persuade effectively, but to persuade truthfully when governments use clear standards for openness. publishing data, citing sources, and correcting errors promptly. They align persuasion with truth. The habit does not weaken authority. it stabilizes it by reducing conflict and building consent.

Section 3 – Citizens and Civic Responsibility

Citizens are not passive recipients of persuasion. They are participants. Their ethical duty lies in testing the claims they encounter, demanding reasons, and resisting manipulation. In a democracy, persuasion cannot function properly unless citizens habitually discern. The Sophists argued that anyone trained in rhetoric could persuade a crowd. This is both empowering and dangerous. Without trained judgment, citizens may fall prey to pleasing speech that lacks substance.

Plato's warning becomes relevant here: relativism not only breeds contradiction. also allows deception to pose as truth.^2 If citizens accept persuasion uncritically, the line between truth and falsehood collapses. Civic duty, therefore, requires active engagement. Citizens must weigh claims against evidence, recognize framing techniques, and distinguish emotional appeals from rational argument.

The task is demanding, but democracy cannot function without it. Aristotle's account of rhetoric assumes that audiences are capable of testing arguments against reason.^3 Modern challenges heighten this burden. Social media floods citizens with information, much of it unverified.

Echo chambers boost one perspective while muting others. In such a setting, the pressure to accept easy truths grows strong. Yet the ethical obligation of citizens is to resist convenience in favor of scrutiny. Education plays a central role. Citizens can be trained. much like the students of Protagoras. to hear both sides, to test arguments, and to seek coherence rather than contradiction.^5^6

Ethical citizenship is not passive consumption but active discernment. Without it, persuasion turns into manipulation, and democracy drifts toward spectacle rather than deliberation. Communities can support this duty by creating spaces for reasoned disagreement: public forums, debate programs, and civic curricula that reward careful evidence. These practices do not remove persuasion. They civilize it by aligning it with shared standards of truth.

Section 4 – Should Persuasion Be Restrained by Principle?

Persuasion is a necessary feature of democratic life. The question is not whether it should exist but whether it must be restrained by principle. To allow persuasion free of principle is to invite conflict. Plato warned against relativism. treating every argument as equally valid. destroys the foundation of truth.^2

Contradictions eventually wear down trust, leaving only performance without substance. Restraint by principle does not mean silencing persuasion. Rather, it means guiding persuasion by fairness, evidence, and civic duty. When arguments are tested against shared principles, persuasion strengthens democracy rather than undermines it.

Aristotle's model. logos, ethos, pathos. already points toward such a guide. Persuasion becomes ethical when it rests on logic, character, and careful emotion, not on deception or spectacle.^3 The modern polis faces this dilemma acutely. Misinformation campaigns, twisted images, and performative politics demonstrate persuasion without rules by principle.

These practices persuade effectively in the short term but wear down truth in the long run. A consistent relativism culminates in contradiction: citizens are convinced yet deceived.[7] Restraining persuasion by principle demands public and social supports. Media must enforce standards of verification. Governments must reward candor over expedience. Citizens must value truth over convenience.

Together, these supports can guide persuasion without silencing it. The goal is not to diminish persuasion but to elevate it. When restrained by principle, persuasion turns a tool of civic education, sharpening judgment rather than clouding it. Without such restraint, persuasion falls into spectacle. appealing but hollow. The choice lies with the polis: principle or conflict. Principled persuasion aligns with the best of the classical tradition: speech that seeks what is true and just, tested in a forum that values reasons over noise.[3]

Conclusion: Ethics as Guardrail for Persuasion
Elections and debates will always be contests of persuasion. The question is whether those contests serve truth or undermine it. Plato's warning remains urgent: relativism breeds contradiction, and contradiction wears down trust in both speech and

speaker.^2 If media, government, and citizens abandon principle, persuasion turns self-defeating.

Yet the story need not end there. Aristotle's guidance offers a path forward. Persuasion can be disciplined by logic, character, and evidence.^3 Media can uphold clarity, government can habit candor, and citizens can demand accountability.

When these actors embrace principle, persuasion aligns with truth rather than opposing it. The ethics of truth in the modern polis are not abstract ideals but practical guardrails. They determine whether persuasion educates or deceives, whether rhetoric builds community or wears it down. Ethics is not an option but a necessity. Without it, persuasion breaks into conflict. With it, persuasion can become the lifeblood of a democratic polis committed to truth.^7

Endnotes

1. Plato, Theaetetus, 152a.

2. Plato, Gorgias.

3. Aristotle, Rhetoric, Book I, chs. 1–2.

4. Kathleen Hall Jamieson, Packaging the Presidency: A History and Criticism of Presidential Campaign Advertising (Oxford University Press, 1996).

5. G. B. Kerferd, The Sophistic Movement (Cambridge University Press, 1981).

6. Edward Schiappa, Protagoras and Logos: A Study in Greek Philosophy and Rhetoric (University of South Carolina Press, 1991).

7. Barbara Cassin, Sophistical Practice: Toward a Consistent Relativism (Fordham University Press, 2014)

Chapter 12

The Sophist and the Question of Truth

Section 1 – The Sophist Speaks

Protagoras claimed that man is the measure of all things. In this view, truth is not an absolute waiting to be discovered but an agreement formed by perception. Lies are not empty falsehoods but rival framings that succeed or fail by persuasion. The Sophist holds that civic life depends on this exchange—persuasion is not corruption, but the essence of the city.

Section 2 – The Shadow of Plato

Thus, Plato's suspicion of the Sophists was inseparable from his political vision. For him, the health of the city required that speech serve truth rather than mere victory. His legacy has defined much of Western philosophy, framing the Sophists as opponents of reasoned inquiry rather than participants in it.

Plato also feared that Sophistic relativism undermined the unity of justice. If every perception is true, then conflicting claims cannot be resolved, leaving society vulnerable to manipulation by the most skilled speakers rather than the wisest leaders. In this sense, rhetoric becomes a weapon in the struggle for power, detached from the pursuit of the good.

His pragmatic reconciliation of rhetoric and truth influenced Roman orators, Christian theologians, and Renaissance humanists. The balance he struck between persuasion and principle has continued to shape discourse across centuries, providing an alternative to Plato's stark rejection of Sophistic influence.

For Aristotle, rhetoric had to remain tied to dialectic and truth. Persuasion divorced from reason was sophistry; persuasion informed by reason was philosophy applied to civic life. In this way, he both preserved the strengths of Sophistic practice and disciplined them through logic and ethics.

Together, these thinkers illustrate the enduring relevance of the Sophists. Far from being historical curiosities, they anticipate modern debates about relativism, postmodernism, and the role of discourse in shaping reality. Their challenge remains: if truth is partly constructed by language and power, how do we safeguard justice against manipulation?

Foucault's contribution sharpened the modern echo by tying truth to institutional power. He demonstrated how schools, courts, and sciences establish regimes of truth—frameworks that decide what counts as knowledge. In this way, he extended the Sophists' insight, showing how persuasion and authority remain inseparable in modern societies.

Barbara Cassin has gone further in defending the Sophists, particularly in her work Sophistical Practice. She argues that the Sophists reveal the flexibility of language and expose the limits of systems that claim to capture truth once and for all. To her, the Sophistic play of discourse is not corruption but a form of intellectual freedom.

Richard Rorty, for instance, emphasized a pragmatist approach that echoed the Sophists' relativism. For Rorty, truth was not a mirror of reality but what worked in practice—an evolving consensus shaped by human needs. This position paralleled Protagoras's claim that man is the measure of all things, suggesting that usefulness, not absolutes, determines validity.

Central to Aristotle's treatment was his division of persuasion into ethos, pathos, and logos. Ethos appealed to the credibility of the speaker, pathos to the emotions of the audience, and logos to rational argument. By identifying these elements, Aristotle created a framework that endures in modern education, law, and politics.

Aristotle's acceptance of rhetoric reflected his pragmatic spirit. Unlike Plato, he did not seek to banish rhetoric from philosophy but to refine it. He defined rhetoric, in essence, as the skill of discerning, in any situation, the persuasive options available—an approach that gave the discipline a clear, systematic purpose. Rhetoric was not an enemy of truth but a practical art that could serve truth when properly guided.

The Phaedrus deepens this critique by presenting rhetoric as a double-edged sword. On one hand, it has the power to stir the soul; on the other, it can deceive if not grounded in knowledge of truth. Plato insisted that rhetoric must be joined with philosophy; otherwise, it risks manipulating citizens and corrupting the soul of the polis.

Plato's rejection of Sophistic rhetoric was not merely abstract but rooted in his dialogues. In the Gorgias, for example, he argues that rhetoric, when practiced without concern for justice, becomes a form of flattery, pleasing the audience without guiding them toward truth. This distinction between dialectic and rhetoric was central to his suspicion: dialectic sought the eternal forms, whereas rhetoric sought only persuasion.

Plato looked upon this with deep suspicion. To him, rhetoric untethered from truth was mere flattery—pleasing without teaching. Relativism, he argued, breeds contradiction: if every claim is valid, none can hold. In the Sophists, he saw not teachers of wisdom, but merchants of opinion, threatening the justice of the polis.

Section 3 – Aristotle's Balance

Aristotle admitted rhetoric into philosophy but demanded it remain tied to reason. He outlined persuasion as threefold: logos (reason), ethos (character), and pathos (emotion). Unlike Protagoras, Aristotle held that truth could be tested, examined, and defended. Persuasion, in his balance, became not the enemy of truth, but its necessary companion when guided by evidence.

Section 4 – The Modern Echo

Later philosophers found themselves returning to the Sophists. Some, like Richard Rorty, valued their pragmatism. Others, like Barbara Cassin, defended the Sophistic play of language as a challenge to rigid systems. Foucault exposed the ties between truth and power, echoing the Sophistic insight that what societies call true is often what institutions enforce. Yet many also stood with Plato, warning that when performance replaces truth, justice collapses.

Section 5 – Perspectives of Five Major Philosophers

Cicero (106–43 BCE)

Cicero, the Roman orator and philosopher, stood at the intersection of Greek philosophy and Roman politics. Trained in the traditions of Plato and Aristotle yet devoted to public life, Cicero understood persuasion as both a civic necessity and a moral art. For him, rhetoric was not an ornament but a tool by which justice could be defended in the forum and senate. He admired eloquence, but he tied it firmly to wisdom, arguing that the orator must also be a philosopher.

To Cicero, the Sophists would appear incomplete. They had mastered speech, but they did not always wed their eloquence to the service of virtue. He acknowledged their brilliance in teaching argument and form, but he feared that technique without moral grounding would corrupt the very republic rhetoric was meant to serve. In his view, eloquence divorced from justice becomes dangerous, for it arms demagogues with weapons against the people.

Yet Cicero was not dismissive. He valued the practical skills of persuasion and knew that in civic life, truth without eloquence is powerless. The Sophists had, in his eyes, safeguarded democracy by teaching citizens how to speak, but they also endangered it by loosening the bond between speech and principle. Thus, Cicero would likely admire their training while insisting that persuasion must always bend toward virtue.

In Cicero's Rome, where politics could mean life or death, persuasion was essential. But unlike the Sophists, Cicero demanded that the orator serve more than victory—he must also serve justice. This balance defined his legacy as one who sought to harmonize philosophy with rhetoric.

Augustine of Hippo (354–430 CE)

Augustine began his life as a student and teacher of rhetoric. Before his conversion to Christianity, he was skilled in the very arts the Sophists cherished: eloquence, persuasion, and debate. But his later writings reveal a deep suspicion of rhetoric when severed from divine truth. For Augustine, words without reference to God were empty shadows. They could move crowds, but they could not save souls.

The Sophists, he would argue, mistook human perception for truth. By making man the measure of all things, they relativized what ought to be absolute, the eternal truths of God. Lies, in their scheme, became merely failed persuasions. For Augustine, this was intolerable. A lie was a sin because it departed from divine truth. No rhetorical skill could transform falsehood into righteousness.

Yet Augustine's critique is not merely rejection. He recognized that rhetoric itself is not evil. Properly directed, it could be a servant of truth. His own writings, especially Confessions and The City of God, demonstrate eloquence of the highest order. He did not abandon rhetoric; he redeemed it, making it serve faith. In this sense, he reshaped the Sophistic craft into a theological tool, reuniting persuasion with eternal truth.

Thus, Augustine's response to the Sophists would be both sharp and transformative. He would condemn their relativism as spiritually dangerous, yet he would also acknowledge the enduring power of their art, provided it is anchored in God. To Augustine, rhetoric without truth was corruption; with truth, it became salvation.

Immanuel Kant (1724–1804)
Kant, writing in the Enlightenment, defined philosophy as the pursuit of reason grounded in universality. For him, morality was not relative but categorical, binding on all rational beings. Truth, likewise, was not contingent on perception but rooted in necessity. The Sophists, in Kant's framework, would represent a misuse of reason: cleverness without principle.

In the Critique of Pure Reason and his moral philosophy, Kant rejected any approach that reduced truth to mere appearance. Persuasion divorced from rational principle was, to him, manipulation. Lies, no matter how convincing, violated the categorical imperative, for they could never be universalized without contradiction. A society that embraces Sophistic relativism would collapse into chaos, as each individual measures truth by convenience rather than law.

Yet Kant would also see the Sophists as revealing an important danger: the human tendency to confuse persuasion with truth. Their emphasis on perception, though flawed, highlighted a temptation reason must resist. For this reason, he would treat the Sophists not merely as opponents but as warnings, examples of what happens when intellect is guided by expedience rather than principle.

Perhaps the lesson is not to banish rhetoric but to discipline it—to insist, as Cicero and Aristotle did, that persuasion must be wedded to virtue. The task of philosophy, then, is not to deny the power of speech but to ensure that speech serves something higher than victory. This is the unfinished legacy of the Sophists.

In today's world of media saturation and polarized politics, the Sophistic question is as urgent as ever. When narratives compete for dominance, truth risks being drowned out by sheer force of repetition. The Sophists remind us that rhetoric is powerful, but also perilous, if left without guiding principles.

The warnings of Plato, the balance of Aristotle, the pragmatism of Cicero and Rorty, the theology of Augustine, and the critiques of Kant, Nietzsche, and Foucault all testify to the Sophists' enduring significance. Each thinker has had to wrestle with the same challenge: can persuasion ever be trusted to serve justice without corrupting it?

Looking back from antiquity through modernity, the Sophists emerge as more than controversial teachers. They appear as the originators of a dilemma that still haunts philosophy: the tension between persuasion and truth. Every era has revisited their insights, whether to condemn them, adapt them, or defend them.

Kant's answer to the Sophists would be stern: rhetoric must never override reason. To persuade without truth is not simply an error, it is an ethical violation. Unlike Aristotle, who sought balance, Kant offered a categorical prohibition: lies, distortions, and relativism have no place in the moral life of the polis.

Friedrich Nietzsche (1844–1900)
Nietzsche, in contrast, would find something to admire in the Sophists. His suspicion of absolute truth led him to describe truths as illusions we have forgotten are illusions—a mobile army of metaphors. In this sense, the Sophists were honest. They admitted that what societies call truth is often a matter of power, perception, and persuasion.

To Nietzsche, Plato's condemnation of the Sophists was less philosophy than politics: an attempt to discredit rivals who threatened his vision of eternal forms. Nietzsche would argue that the Sophists revealed a deeper truth—that there are no truths beyond perspectives. Lies are not absolute errors but competing narratives. In this sense, the Sophists anticipated his perspectivism, the claim that all knowledge arises from a standpoint.

Yet Nietzsche did not see this as license for weakness. He valued strength, vitality, and the creative will. The Sophists, by exposing the plasticity of truth, empowered individuals to shape meaning rather than submit to dogma. For him, the danger was not relativism but the denial of it—the pretense, exemplified by Plato and Christianity, that eternal truths exist beyond human creation.

Thus Nietzsche would stand as one of the Sophists' most unlikely allies. He would not romanticize them as noble sages, but he would admire their audacity in rejecting absolutes. To Nietzsche, the Sophists were closer to realists than deceivers: they embraced the play of power and language that underlies all human claims to truth.

Michel Foucault (1926–1984)

Foucault, like Nietzsche, distrusted claims of objective truth. He explored how knowledge is bound to power, how institutions create the conditions under which some statements are accepted as true while others are dismissed. In this respect, he saw in the Sophists a precursor to his own project.

For Foucault, the Sophists revealed that truth is not discovered in isolation but negotiated within structures of power. Their relativism, far from being a flaw, exposed a hidden reality: that persuasion and authority determine what societies call true. Lies, in this framework, are not absolute errors but failed bids for recognition.

Yet Foucault also understood Plato's warning. When all is reduced to power, contradiction emerges. Systems that enforce truth also produce resistance, and every regime of knowledge eventually undermines itself. This tension echoes Plato's fear of relativism but without returning to absolutes. For Foucault, the Sophists had unmasked the play of power, but they had not solved it.

In the modern polis, Foucault would see Sophistic strategies at work in media, government, and even scientific discourse. His reaction would not be to condemn them but to analyze them: to show how persuasion operates beneath claims of neutrality. Thus, he would both validate and extend the Sophistic project, situating it within the genealogy of truth and power.

Section 6 – Closing Reflection
The Sophists were neither villains nor heroes. They revealed a hard fact: persuasion mediates what societies call truth. Yet without principles, persuasion decays into manipulation. Perhaps the real danger is not that Sophists relativize truth, but that communities fail to set boundaries for persuasion. The challenge remains: can rhetoric serve truth without becoming its enemy?

Endnotes

1. Plato's critique of rhetoric as flattery appears in Gorgias 463a–466a, where he distinguishes rhetoric from true art. See also Phaedrus 259e–261a, on rhetoric joined with knowledge.

2. Aristotle discusses rhetoric as a counterpart to dialectic in Rhetoric I.1 (1354a). His tripartite division of persuasion into ethos, pathos, and logos is found in Rhetoric I.2 (1356a).

3. Richard Rorty's pragmatism redefines truth in terms of what a community permits us to say. See Rorty, Philosophy and the Mirror of Nature (Princeton University Press, 1979).

4. Barbara Cassin develops a defense of the Sophists in Sophistical Practice: Toward a Consistent Relativism (Fordham University Press, 2014).

5. Michel Foucault's notion of 'regimes of truth' is discussed in Power/Knowledge: Selected Interviews and Other Writings, 1972–1977 (Pantheon Books, 1980)

Chapter 13
The Measure of All Things Today: The Sophist and the Philosopher in a Networked World

This chapter returns to the two figures who have guided the book from the start: the Sophist, represented here most clearly by Protagoras, and the Philosophers figured by Plato and Aristotle. The Sophist reminds us that persuasion is not an ornament added to civic life but one of its basic structures.

The Philosopher reminds us that without standards beyond mere persuasion, the search for truth is at risk of dissolving into performance. In our own time, of feeds, metrics, micro-audiences, and recommendation systems, their conversation has not ended; it has simply migrated to new stages. Our task is to ask how Protagoras' famous claim, "man is the measure of all things," works in a plural, networked society, and what ethical guardrails the Philosopher's tradition would place on modern persuasion. [1–5, 6–7]

1) Re-centering the Sophist and the Philosopher
Protagoras' thesis—reported and examined in Plato's dialogues, places the human participant at the center of judgment. Truth, at least in matters of perception and civic deciding, emerges within practice: within the speech, institutions, and habits by which a city weighs claims.

Plato's Protagoras and Theaetetus bring the slogan to life; his Gorgias carries the reply, warning that persuasion can become flattery when it forgets knowledge. Aristotle, rather than rejecting rhetoric, disciplines it as the art of finding the available means of persuasion in each case, provided speech aims at truth and serves deliberation. [1–4]

Those classical coordinates still orient us. The Sophist marks persuasion's inevitability and civic value; the Philosopher marks persuasion's limits and duties. Our contemporary question is not whether persuasion structures public life—it does—but how to keep that structure from collapsing into manipulation when speed, scale, and incentives change.

2) "Man is the Measure" in a Plural Society

Protagoras' measure-doctrine can be read as a charter for pluralism: in diverse societies, people encounter the world through different traditions, vocabularies, and experiences. No single standpoint captures the whole.

This awareness is a civic strength. It tempers dogmatism, encourages humility, and invites negotiation among groups that must live together. The modern gains are obvious: freedom of conscience, protection for minority views, and practices of public justification in which reasons are offered to those who disagree. [1–2, 6–7]

But pluralism has a threshold. If we treat all claims as equally warranted because each speaks from a perspective, standards for evidence and correction can fade. Plato's old worry returns: without a discipline of truth, the most fluent speakers—or the loudest networks—can become de facto arbiters of reality. Aristotle's way through is still instructive: keep rhetoric, but tether it to sound inference, credible evidence, and ethical purpose. [3–4, 5]

3) Dissoi Logoi Meets the Attention Economy

The Sophists trained citizens in dissoi logoi—double arguments—so that opposing cases could be heard before judgment. The ideal presumes an arena where arguments can meet, answer, and improve one another. Modern media retain that ideal in form—interviews, op-eds, debates, comment sections, but the underlying economics often reward a different habit: rapid amplification of arresting claims. When attention is monetized, friction that would normally slow persuasion (asking for sources, sitting with counter-evidence) is treated as a cost rather than a civic safeguard.

Empirical research underscores the tension. False stories tend to diffuse faster and farther online than true ones, in part because novelty and emotion drive sharing; exposure patterns are shaped by ranking systems and the choices of homophilous networks; and long-term consumption of news via platforms can both broaden and narrow exposure depending on user behavior and design choices. None of these findings doom public reason, but they confirm that the stagecraft of attention can tilt the field against dissoi logoi if we are careless. [10–15]

4) Editorial Chains and the Ethics of Credibility

In many outlets, a two-step pattern has become common: a news frame that selects what is salient, followed by commentary that ratifies the frame. The sequence is not inherently corrupt—analysis has always accompanied reporting, but it can blur the difference between evidence and endorsement.

The antidote is the same one Aristotle urged: make the warrants visible. Who is the source? How was the claim verified? What counter-evidence was considered but set aside? Modern journalism has articulated such standards in part, verification, independence, transparency—not to drain speech of persuasion but to discipline persuasion in service of truth. Fact-checking is the institutional cousin of dissoi logoi, though often noticeably biased: it stages a counter-case where error can be corrected without humiliation. [8–9]

5) Platforms, Algorithms, and the Measure of the Feed

If the measure of truth is set inside civic practice, then platform design is not neutral. Ranking choices, recommendation objectives, and interface cues shape what appears credible, what travels, and what becomes common knowledge. Research on large-scale recommender systems shows how small shifts in objective functions can dramatically alter what users encounter; design can widen or narrow the range of views, reward or penalize extreme content, and influence the tempo of controversy.

To put it in classical terms: the agora now has an architect. The ethics of that architecture, transparency of criteria, avenues for appeal, guardrails against amplification of obvious falsehoods, belong squarely within the Philosopher's (Plato and Aristotle), demand that persuasion be answerable to knowledge. [12–15, 10–11]

6) Three Contemporary Arenas for the Sophist–Philosopher Dialogue
Elections and Public Deliberation.

Campaigns have always been theaters of persuasion. What has changed is granularity and speed. Micro-segmented messaging, influencer networks, and real-time A/B testing let campaigns discover which phrases mobilize which subgroups. From a Sophistic angle, this is simply refined audience adaptation; from the Philosopher's angle, (Plato and Aristotle), it raises questions about fairness and mutual accountability. Healthy practice keeps two commitments in view:

messaging grounded in checkable facts, and civic forums where competing claims must meet in public, not only in tailored streams. [8, 10–12, 16–17]

Public Health and Collective Risk.

Where the stakes involve shared risk, the cost of performative speech is high. Here, the Sophist's gift, translating technical knowledge into accessible narratives, must be paired with visible methods and open data so that dissenters can audit claims rather than simply distrust them. Disinformation thrives where institutions hide their workings; transparency turns persuasion from "trust me" into "check me." [10, 16]

AI as a New Speaker.

Systems that generate text, images, and video at scale introduce a novel actor into civic persuasion. The Sophist would recognize their power to adapt language to audience; the Philosophers (Plato and Aristotle), would ask how we ensure provenance, prevent impersonation, and maintain avenues for challenge.

The practical answer echoes classical themes: provenance markers and disclosure, auditable training data when claims of fact are made, and design choices that slow the viral spread of content flagged as likely false while preserving avenues for correction. The point is not to ban persuasion by machines but to subject it to the same ethical discipline we demand of human speakers. [10, 16]

7) Guardrails: A Civic Ethic for Persuasion

What would a Protagorean city, instructed by Plato and Aristotle, require of modern persuasion? At least six guardrails follow.

1) Transparency of warrants.

Claims of fact should carry visible links to evidence and methods such as, documents, data, procedures of verification—so that citizens can test assertions. This is Aristotle's logos anchored in auditability, not merely eloquence. [4, 8–9]

2) Contestability by design.

Platforms and institutions should make it easy to see counter-arguments and to surface reputable challenges. Dissoi logoi needs a user interface. [6–7, 12–15]

3) Proportional amplification.

High-reach systems should throttle demonstrably false or decontextualized claims while preserving traceable paths for correction and appeal. The aim is not censorship but calibration: reducing harms of speed while maintaining avenues for truth to travel. [10–11, 16]

4) Character and accountability.

Cicero and Quintilian insisted that good speech requires good character. In modern terms: disclose conflicts, label advocacy, separate reporting from opinion, and make corrections conspicuous. Credibility is not a vibe; it is a set of visible habits. [18, 8]

5) Education for judgment.

Rhetorical literacy—spotting framing, testing sources, practicing double arguments, belongs in civic education alongside statistics and basic logic. A public that can perform dissoi logoi is harder to fool and easier to persuade responsibly. [6–7, 17]

6) Friction where speed misleads.

When evidence shows that certain kinds of content predictably exploit attention (for example, emotionally charged falsehoods), institutions should introduce thoughtful friction, cool-down intervals, pre-publication prompts, or "read before share" nudges, so that judgment can catch up with reaction. Slowness, at the right moment, is an ethical technology. [10–11, 16]

8) Reconciling the Sophist's Optimism with the Philosopher's Demands

Protagoras was not a cynic. He believed that skillful speech could improve civic life, teaching people to deliberate, to foresee consequences, to compare alternatives. The modern world vindicates that hope every day in classrooms, courts, and councils that depend on persuasion to convert expertise into judgment.

But Protagoras also needs Plato at the table, reminding us that eloquence can outpace evidence, and Aristotle in the chair, asking that we show our work. The union of these three is not a compromise with truth; it is a way for truth to survive modern speed.

Conclusion: The Dialogue That Must Not End
The Sophist and the Philosophers, (Plato and Aristotle), have argued for twenty-five centuries because each sees something the other risks forgetting. The Sophist sees that people must be moved before they can be taught; the Philosophers, sees that people must be taught before they can be trusted to be moved. In a networked world, their dialogue is not a museum piece. It is a design brief for institutions, platforms, and classrooms. If "man is the measure," then our shared practices—verification, transparency, contestation—are the rulers by which we will continue to measure truth and lies. The work is permanent, which is to say, it is ours. [1–5, 8–11, 16–17]

Endnotes
1. Plato, Theaetetus 151e–152a, on Protagoras' "man is the measure" doctrine.

2. Plato, Protagoras 320d–329d, on civic instruction and the teachability of virtue.

3. Plato, Gorgias 463a–466a, on rhetoric as flattery when severed from knowledge.

4. Aristotle, Rhetoric I.2 (1355b25–26), defining rhetoric as the capacity to find the available means of persuasion.

5. Aristotle, Metaphysics IV.7 (1011b25), on truth as saying of what is that it is, and of what is not that it is not.

6. G. B. Kerferd, The Sophistic Movement (Cambridge University Press, 1981), on Sophistic methods including antilogikē.

7. Rosamond Kent Sprague, ed., The Older Sophists (Hackett, 2001), selections on dissoi logoi and Gorgias' "Encomium of Helen."

8. Bill Kovach and Tom Rosenstiel, The Elements of Journalism (Crown, various editions), on verification, independence, and transparency.

9. Lucas Graves, Deciding What's True: The Rise of Political Fact-Checking in American Journalism (Oxford University Press, 2016).

10. David M. J. Lazer et al., "The science of fake news," Science 359, no. 6380 (2018): 1094–1096.

11. Soroush Vosoughi, Deb Roy, and Sinan Aral, "The spread of true and false news online," Science 359, no. 6380 (2018): 1146–1151.

12. Seth Flaxman, Sharad Goel, and Justin M. Rao, "Filter Bubbles, Echo Chambers, and Online News Consumption," Public Opinion Quarterly 80, no. S1 (2016): 298–320.

13. Eytan Bakshy, Solomon Messing, and Lada A. Adamic, "Exposure to ideologically diverse news and opinion on Facebook," Science 348, no. 6239 (2015): 1130–1132.

14. Paul Covington, Jay Adams, and Emre Sargin, "Deep Neural Networks for YouTube Recommendations," Proceedings of the 10th ACM Conference on Recommender Systems (RecSys '16), 2016.

15. Claire Wardle and Hossein Derakhshan, "Information Disorder: Toward an interdisciplinary framework for research and policy making," Council of Europe report, 2017.

16. Cass R. Sunstein, #Republic: Divided Democracy in the Age of Social Media (Princeton University Press, 2017).

17. Eli Pariser, The Filter Bubble: What the Internet Is Hiding from You (Penguin, 2011).

18. Quintilian, Institutio Oratoria XII.1.1, on the orator as vir bonus dicendi peritus (a good person skilled in speaking).

19. Christof Rapp, "Aristotle's Rhetoric," Stanford Encyclopedia of Philosophy (rev. ed.), for background on aims and methods of rhetoric.

www.ingramcontent.com/pod-product-compliance
Lightning Source LLC
Chambersburg PA
CBHW060504280326
41933CB00014B/2858